On the Market

D0851811

On the Market

Strategies for a Successful Academic Job Search

Sandra L. Barnes

LYNNE
RIENNER
PUBLISHERS

BOULDER
LONDON

Published in the United States of America in 2007 by
Lynne Rienner Publishers, Inc.
1800 30th Street, Boulder, Colorado 80301
www.rienner.com

and in the United Kingdom by
Lynne Rienner Publishers, Inc.
3 Henrietta Street, Covent Garden, London WC2E 8LU

Library of Congress Cataloging-in-Publication Data
Barnes, Sandra L.
On the market : strategies for a successful academic job search / Sandra L. Barnes.
    p. cm.
    Includes index.
ISBN-13: 978-1-58826-511-1 (hardcover : alk. paper)
ISBN-13: 978-1-58826-535-7 (pbk. : alk. paper)
    1. College teachers. 2. College teaching—Vocational guidance. I. Title.
LB1778.B37 2007
378.1'2023—dc22

        2006037828

British Cataloguing in Publication Data
A Cataloguing in Publication record for this book
is available from the British Library.

Printed and bound in the United States of America

The paper used in this publication meets the requirements
of the American National Standard for Permanence of
Paper for Printed Library Materials Z39.48-1992.

5 4 3 2 1

Contents

Illustrations

Acknowledgments

This book would not have been possible without the input of a variety of academics and graduate students. First and foremost, I thank Jacqueline Boles, professor emeritus at Georgia State University, whose interest in teaching portfolios was the impetus for this work. Special thanks also to Dawn Baunach, Nandi Crosby, Jim Ainsworth-Darnell, and Charles Gallagher for their invaluable suggestions to me as I entered the job market; their ideas have been incorporated here. For their comments and review of documents that later became part of this book, I am very grateful to the senior faculty at Georgia State University: Charles Jaret, Toshi Kii, Ralph LaRossa, and Kirk Elifson. Additional thanks to Juan Battle for his enhancements to my original publishing flowchart. Special thanks to the anonymous reviewers for reading the early draft of the book. Finally, many thanks to Clara Brown for her wisdom and encouragement, and for reminding me of the need to consider crucial nonacademic issues that can profoundly impact one's ability to select the best career path based on professional and personal objectives.

—*Sandra L. Barnes*

1

Introduction

Entering the academic job market can be an exciting time. It can also be quite harrowing. Although graduate students may be excited about finding a tenure-track position or that prestigious postdoctoral fellowship, many are also nervous about competition, completing the dissertation, graduating, and beginning an employment process that can be quite overwhelming. *On the Market: Strategies for a Successful Academic Job Search* is a guide to help the reader successfully identify, apply for, compete for, and get a tenure-track position in academia. This resource is a hands-on approach to organizing each step of the process from pre-application to job acceptance.

This book examines professional and personal issues every candidate should think about before entering or re-entering the job market, or when considering, accepting, or rejecting a position. Included are suggestions, practical strategies, "quick lists," publishing strategies, and advice from faculty, as well as observations and ideas developed during my personal employment search process. Chapters 2–7 focus on professional issues and Chapters 8 and 9 on personal ones. I contend that a comprehensive search must consider both of these important arenas. Although no resource can guarantee a successful search, utilizing the material contained in this volume will increase a candidate's chances of finding an academic position that meets her or his professional and personal needs.

Chapters 2, 3, and 4 focus on maximizing the graduate school experience and developing a competitive, comprehensive application packet, as well as how to respond to advertisements, garner letters of recommendation, and develop a curriculum vita. I also provide a proposed timeline, to be used while in graduate school, to organize and schedule important milestones in the employment search and map each phase of the process.

Chapter 5 addresses one of the most important resources to distinguish yourself from other candidates—the teaching portfolio. In the past, teaching portfolios were required primarily for candidates applying at comprehensive liberal arts institutions or teaching colleges. This is not so today—many institutions now require a teaching portfolio as part of the application packet. To be more competitive, you should know how to create this important documentation of your teaching experience. Chapter 6 specifically addresses issues related to interviewing, including how to organize an on-campus academic presentation and teaching demonstration, as well as social dynamics to consider during onsite visits and when negotiating employment offers. Other academic and nontraditional job opportunities are examined in Chapter 7. A variety of personal or nonacademic issues that should be considered before accepting a position are included in Chapter 8. Candidates often overlook this area and it can dramatically influence their quality of life after a position has been accepted. Topics include how to assess the campus and departmental climate and balancing professional and personal considerations. Chapter 9 examines topics of interest specifically for racial or ethnic minorities, women, older or single persons, and candidates planning to relocate to unfamiliar regions. These nontraditional or underrepresented groups are entering the academic market in increasing numbers and their often-unique considerations have not been addressed in other books about the academic employment search. Chapter 10 includes information for junior faculty who are interested in re-entering the job market prior to tenure. Throughout the book, I also include suggestions, ideas, and anecdotal information to expedite the employment process.

This book has been developed to reduce the anxiety associated with entering the academic job market. Because there are a variety of issues to consider when applying for a position in academia, many people may feel overwhelmed. Others may feel competent about applying, but are not sure about the appropriate steps to take. And even those for whom applying and interviewing are "old hat" may fail to consider options that might make them more competitive candidates. A variety of problems of scale face graduate students during this period, which is, perhaps, the most important first step in their academic career. Certain oversights may cause minimal negative effects during the application process, while others may have long-term consequences. And junior faculty who are contemplating re-entering the market must also be better informed before and during that process. People who follow a formal, structured, organized process have a better chance at landing a position and may also increase their chances of landing their ideal position.

On the Market incorporates a variety of guidelines to better prepare candidates to enter (or re-enter) the job market, to better inform them about often-overlooked issues, and to expand their knowledge to minimize the challenges associated with a competitive academic market. It is my hope that the reader will benefit from my personal experiences and those of other professors who have successfully located positions in academia.

Readers should consider two important caveats regarding use of this resource. First, although I have attempted to examine many issues central to a successful job search, this resource should not be considered or used as a substitute for locating and establishing relationships with mentors in academia. The wisdom, experiences, and advice of faculty, graduate advisers, and administrators are crucial in both performing a successful job search and having a positive, productive career in academia. *On the Market* was written to be used as a helpful tool to augment information and suggestions provided by seasoned advisers and mentors. Thus this resource should complement rather than compete with human resources in your respective disciplines. Second, readers should note that the academic market can vary considerably by discipline. What might be the case in the social sciences may be less so in the humanities—and irrelevant in the physical and life sciences. Although certain themes are germane regardless of the discipline (for example, the importance of maximizing the graduate experience and performing an organized search), this resource focuses on job search efforts in the social sciences and, to a somewhat lesser degree, the humanities. Again, mentors and graduate advisers will help tailor portions of this resource to meet the specific job search dynamics in your discipline.

On the Market can be a valuable resource for the newly graduated student who is just entering the market, an ABD (all but dissertation) who wishes to begin early preparation, graduate students who are considering nonacademic posts, nonacademics who wish to transition into academic positions, as well as current nontenured academics who are re-entering the market. Competition can be keen and no one is guaranteed a successful job search or that their first position will be ideal, but, with proper preparation and this guide, students and faculty members can maximize their efforts for locating an academic position.

2

The Academic Job Market

The academic market, like any market, can be unpredictable. It experiences a variety of conditions, some expected, some unexpected, that affect job seekers—downturns or upswings in demand based on market conditions, changes in supply and demand based on shifts in the number of graduates in a given year or a surplus of graduates in previous years. While many of these conditions are beyond the control of the employment candidate, you must be aware of those dynamics that can be influenced and what choices you can make to help ensure gainful employment. Anecdotes abound about students who completed their graduate studies, many from prestigious institutions, only to find few or no available positions in their field of study—or those who, for a variety of reasons, found themselves in great demand and were able to obtain several job offers. But most candidates probably find themselves somewhere in between and wish to increase their chances of finding a position. Several general issues should be considered regarding the academic job market.

The well-informed candidate should be aware of the general employment trends in his or her discipline. Information is often available via the Internet by accessing the website of national academic societies (e.g., the Modern Languages Association, American Sociological Association, etc.) or journals such as *The Chronicle of Higher Education* that post yearly employment statistics of graduates in their discipline by categories such as subfield, institution, race/ethnicity, region, and sex. Recent graduates (those who have located positions and those who are still searching) can provide a wealth of information about their employment experiences and prepare you for what should be expected. Also, older faculty members who are active in national and regional conferences and societies are often aware of employment peaks and troughs and how national issues may have affected short-term job prospects. Such people tend to also have historical information about periods when employment in a discipline was limited and how candidates adjusted.

In addition, be aware that employment prospects are conditioned on institutional needs, departmental needs, and budgetary constraints. A college or university may have established short- and long-term goals to expand a certain discipline, combine several departments for budgetary reasons, or develop a new program based on student response. Such changes may dramatically affect the need for new faculty. Academic departments develop goals and objectives that affect faculty needs as well. For example, based on the desire to focus efforts on several disciplinary paths, a department may create new positions for the subsequent year and earmark funds for one or two new positions over the next few years. In such instances, departments may be clear about the type of candidates they are looking for, or they may be searching for candidates with a general level of expertise but with a focus on a new topic or area. Regardless, new employment opportunities often result. However, even with such plans and projections, all institutions must contend with budgetary issues. Just as funds are set aside for certain positions, the search process may be delayed indefinitely due to budgetary revisions and unexpected economic constraints. Understanding these types of issues is important to determine the most appropriate approach to the academic employment market.

■ General Suggestions

Although this book contains a variety of specific suggestions, practical points, and lists to consider, be mindful of several general traits that are needed to be most successful in the academic job market.

• *Commitment.* In many ways, looking for employment can be a full-time job. You must realize at the outset that competing for a position can be time consuming—with no guarantee of the desired outcome. Even the most qualified candidate must contend with application deadlines, timetables, locating references, followup, delays, and bureaucratic issues. You must be committed to the process in order for it to work for you. This will require a great deal of patience and dedication.

• *Organization/discipline.* Depending on available positions and your approach to the job search, you may decide to apply for fifty or more positions (I know people who applied for even more). You must be extremely disciplined, focused, and organized to maintain records of items such as: each institution to which you apply, documents that are sent, time frames for responses, and any special institutional requirements. It is important to develop a structure for organizing and maintaining information on each position and to consistently document each step in the search process (refer to Figure 4.9, the application schedule). Without this level of detail, you are certain to overlook critical deadlines, forget application steps, and fail to submit appropriate documents, all of which undermine successful application.

• *Thoroughness/attention to detail.* Remember the importance of following through on action items and confirming that people involved in the application process (e.g., professors who write letters of recommendation) do so as well. Of equal importance is the need to carefully review and edit all application documents. Although search committees realize that candidates are probably applying for a variety of positions, the content and caliber of an application packet should *suggest* that it is the only one you have submitted.

• *Assertiveness.* A faculty member in the department from which I graduated gave me some good advice. In regard to the job search process, she noted, "When all is said and done, you are the only person who is really looking out for you." This statement may initially seem harsh, but her point was that, as a candidate on the market, I had to take ownership of my search experience. This meant taking responsibility for each step in the process. So while I had to rely on others for certain items, only I would ultimately live with the end result. Thus, be action-oriented and pursue the necessary people and information that will help develop the most complete, impressive application packet.

• *Cooperation/planning.* Although it is easy for candidates to become preoccupied with the many application requirements, you must be mindful that a variety of people are typically needed to successfully apply and that faculty and staff have other responsibilities. This will require you to plan in advance to give people sufficient time to complete requests (e.g., at least two to three weeks notice to write letters of recommendation, review documents, or schedule to attend mock presentations, and one month for schools to generate transcripts). A cooperative attitude will help ensure support and involvement from others.

• *Balance.* In addition to submitting applications, interviewing, and soliciting letters of reference, most candidates will have other graduate responsibilities such as completing the dissertation or serving as a teaching or research assistant. And some will have personal responsibilities associated with having a spouse, partner, or raising children. Although it is difficult to plan for uncertainties (e.g., your child catches a cold the weekend before an interview or key application deadline), other obligations should be proactively considered before and during the search process. For example, if you are a teaching assistant with grading responsibilities, it will be important to plan search activities so they do not conflict with periods after midterm and final exams when you will be expected to grade course papers. Juggling employment and personal commitments will often mean incorporating additional time and contingency plans into the search process, being intentional about the search scope and focus, establishing a committed network of support (e.g., additional childcare help, a trusted peer to take notes for you in a graduate seminar), and notifying faculty in whose classes you assist that you are on the job market.

• *Objectivity.* It is often difficult to objectively critique yourself, but you must acquire this skill if you wish to present the best image during the application and interview process. This means being able to recognize areas for improvement, take constructive criticism from colleagues and peers, and honestly gauge abilities and skills relative to a potential position or employment constraint. Realistically examine your options and make the best decisions based on the information available. For example, this means acknowledging that many candidates may be competing for a limited number of positions and competition for positions at more prestigious institutions will be even stiffer. With this in mind, you may wish to develop specific strategies to increase your competitiveness (e.g., work toward increasing your publications). Objectivity is also required when selecting the "best" position based on a variety of factors, or seeking other options if chances of locating an acceptable position appear slim. Given the difficulty associated with being objective about decisions with long-term implications, it is helpful to seek the advice of objective people (e.g., a dissertation adviser or committee member, a mentor, or a trusted friend).

3

Maximizing the Graduate School Experience

M any students believe that the job search begins at the end of their graduate school experience or after they earn their Ph.D. In actuality, preparing for an effective job search should begin when you enter a graduate program. This statement is not to suggest that you should focus your efforts while in graduate school on locating employment. However, conscientious students should realize the importance of each step in their graduate careers and that some steps can be taken while in graduate school to make them more competitive when entering the job market. Although certain facets of the graduate experience will be influenced and, in some cases, determined by departmental structure, protocol, and needs (e.g., teaching or research assistant posts, dissertation advisers), it is important to recognize those areas of the experience where you have some agency—and proactively shape them to strengthen your employment search endeavors. This chapter focuses on ways you can take advantage of opportunities while in graduate school, important relationships that should be established, and approaches that can be taken to ensure the graduate experience culminates in *both* a Ph.D. and gainful employment.

▩ The Importance of the Graduate Program

Most students enter graduate school to pursue an area of study and become an "expert" on that topic. Those with plans to seek a tenure-track position in academia strive to earn a Ph.D. They

11

expect to spend many hours studying, performing research, and teaching. The Ph.D. objective often results in tunnel vision and hinders some students from availing themselves of a variety of opportunities that could give them a competitive edge when they enter the job arena. For example, you may view a seminar solely in terms of mastering the required readings and earning a good grade, instead of also viewing it as an opportunity to write a paper for publication, collaborate with a professor or fellow peer on research, or pick up teaching pointers from an exceptional instructor. It is important to consider these types of opportunities as well as the immediate demands of a course. This point cannot be emphasized enough!

People should intentionally shift their approach to graduate school from one of student to one of burgeoning scholar. This means that activities such as courses, qualifying exams, research projects, and presentations should be considered building blocks toward a successful dissertation, vita, and, ultimately, employment search rather than merely hoops through which you must jump. The following question should be considered during such experiences—"What do I need to learn from this assignment or activity that will contribute to my development as a scholar or instructor or to my research interests?" In many instances, expanding your approach to graduate school does not require extensive additional effort, and the rewards can be great.

Last, some may debate this point, but the status of the institution and/or graduate program may impact the success of your job search. Just as hierarchies exist in the larger society, they exist in academia as well. Some search committee members may consider the prestige of a certain institution or department (or the reputation of certain faculty) as a broad marker for the caliber of its graduates. If this is the case, candidates from such places have a higher likelihood of selection for interviews and job offers. This does not preclude a successful employment search if you are not matriculating at a prestigious institution; however, knowledge of such tendencies will be important for how you develop your employment strategies. Readers should refer to the timeline (Figure 3.2) at the end of this chapter as a tool in organizing the graduate experience to maximize the job search. The following observations can enhance your graduate school experience in general, and better prepare you for the job market as well.

• *Developing a network.* The connections that are established in graduate school are invaluable as you matriculate and become even more valuable after you begin your career. Interact with as many department members as possible, even people outside your areas of interest. Faculty members can provide a wealth of knowledge and can also become great role models and mentors. Remember that they are already in positions that most graduate students aspire to have. In addition, most professors have existing networks that they can tap into on your behalf. Early in my graduate experience, I submitted a paper for a national conference and was upset when it was not selected for inclusion. I mentioned my disappointment to a faculty member who immediately picked up the telephone, made a few calls, and (while I stood there, mouth agape) located a position for me on a roundtable at the conference. Such a favor would not have been possible had I not established ties with this professor. Developing professional and, in some cases, personal relationships can benefit you later.

• *Getting published.* Seek out as many opportunities to publish academic papers as possible. This means joint research with interested faculty members and fellow classmates or developing articles and ideas on your own. In addition, many faculty members are open to reviewing students' articles before they are submitted as well as suggesting academic journals that are more liberal about considering such submissions. Because of the importance of this topic, it is addressed in detail later in this chapter.

• *Writing letters of recommendation.* Among a large pool of qualified job candidates, the caliber of your letters of recommendation can be the difference between making the "long-short" list, the "short" list, or in getting an interview. Letters from people who know you, your research, and your character can impress search committee members. In some instances, letters from well-established, well-published scholars are considered most impressive. A favorable letter of recommendation from your primary Ph.D. adviser/dissertation committee chairperson will be crucial and expected. Search committees recognize that this person has worked most closely with you during the dissertation process and can assess your abilities, skills, and potential as a burgeoning scholar. Application packets without such a letter will, at the least, be suspect, and usually sabotage your chances of serious consideration.

• *Reviewing application documents.* Faculty members may agree to review and edit your vita, cover letter, or other supporting documents. Such an additional level of review by more experienced academics may uncover errors. As important, faculty members can provide suggestions on ways to improve document content so they are more professional, accurate, and impressive. Be sure to review these documents carefully yourself before providing them to faculty members (drafts with typos and errors will undermine your credibility).

• *Offering advice on career choices.* Faculty members can be an excellent source of advice about career decisions. In some cases, seek out people with similar interests and aspirations. Other times, a "neutral" professor with few ties to your area may be able to provide a different perspective. Remember that such decisions will impact you directly (and not the advising faculty member); however, feedback from a trusted, informed person is often helpful.

• *Critiquing mock presentations and mock interviews.* Not only can faculty members provide suggestions to strengthen your presentation skills, but their time in the discipline makes them an excellent source of information about the types of questions job candidates may encounter. In order to hone your interview skills, faculty members may ask challenging questions or serve as "difficult" attendees to help you become accustomed to interacting with a wide array of people and in pressure-filled, difficult circumstances. You will probably not face such circumstances when interviewing, but it is best to be prepared.

• *Notifying students of job openings.* Faculty members can also take advantage of their existing networks and inform students of job openings that may not be advertised in expected outlets.

• *Critiquing teaching.* Ask one or several faculty members to observe you teaching a course and provide feedback and suggestions. After the evaluation, request an official evaluation letter. This type of assessment adds yet another dimension to a teaching portfolio and may have more credibility than traditional student evaluations.

■ Key People

Although faculty are often quite busy teaching and performing research themselves, some will be open to assisting students they believe are conscientious and prepared. Get to know the professors professionally and, as much as is appropriate, personally. These are the best people to review application documents, critique mock presentations, attend mock interviews, and review papers for publication. So as not to require too much of their time, it may be wise to select people who are most willing to provide assistance and always give them sufficient time to respond. While it is important to cultivate a variety of relationships, ties with the following people are crucial:

• *Graduate director.* Not only does the graduate director have knowledge of every dimension of the graduate program, but that person can also provide information about possible grants, how previous students fared on the job market, strengths of the graduate program that you may wish to highlight in application documents, teaching opportunities, as well as support for conference attendance. Establishing a relationship with the graduate director is the most important link to current information about your program. Remember that the graduate director's responsibility is to help ensure that students are informed about the steps needed to complete the program and to take advantage of what the program has to offer. For example, during my graduate program, the graduate director made me aware of a very competitive dissertation grant in my area of focus. He knew of my interests and felt that I might want to compete—not only would the grant provide extensive funding to complete the dissertation, but it would add another important dimension to my vita (obtaining outside funding). I applied for the grant and, with the help of members of the department and the graduate director, was selected. This opportunity would not have been possible without the graduate director's assistance.

• *Dissertation chairperson and committee members.* Of all the department members, the people on your dissertation committee are most informed about your research, the progress you are making, and the best ways to eventually "market" you as a candidate.

It is also expected that committee members will write letters of reference (refer to Chapter 4 for more details). As noted earlier, search committees may view candidates suspiciously if their letters of reference do not include recommendations from one (preferably the chairperson) or all of the people on their dissertation committee. Your committee may also provide publication suggestions for converting the dissertation into a monograph or a series of articles. Consider your dissertation committee carefully. Be mindful that the ability to actually select committee members will vary by department. Some students are able to solicit faculty members directly, others provide input to their dissertation committee chairperson, and some have very little control over committee constitution. However, the goal is to work with people who are knowledgeable about your research subject, interested in your work, and who can help strengthen you as an academician. Faculty who are interested in your personal well-being and growth as a well-rounded scholar are also ideal. While "stars" in the discipline may be assets to a committee, they may be too busy to provide the necessary (and timely) feedback for the project. In some cases, newer faculty members may have great new ideas and insight because they are often more likely to be abreast of the most recent research in the area. If possible, it is ideal to have a diverse committee of older faculty as well as newer members in the department who work well with you and each other. Ask your graduate director for recommendations.

• *Department chairperson or head.* In addition to approving funding for conferences, teaching assistantships, and other departmental support, the department chairperson/head may be an excellent source of advice about locating employment. Also, a letter of recommendation from the chairperson can enhance your application packet. Typically the chairperson has had numerous years in the discipline, is well published, and has also established an extensive network. Many may be willing to share these resources with you. Certain suggestions can be quite beneficial. For example, during my final year in graduate school, I had to decide whether to rush and attempt to complete the dissertation in order to graduate in June of that year or to wait and graduate in December. Of course, following the traditional process, I wanted to graduate in June. I also had two tenure-track job offers that seemed exciting and interesting. I sought advice from several faculty members, including the department chairperson. He objectively presented the pros and cons of each graduation option and noted several important considerations for delaying graduation until December. Such a strategy would mean that I would not start a tenure-track post until the following year. However, this option would provide me with an additional semester to focus on interviewing more thoroughly, convert my dissertation into academic articles, and take a much-needed rest before I began my career. Because I would graduate midyear, the tenure "clock" would not begin until I started work the following fall. After weighing my options, I elected to delay graduation, and the benefits were tremendous. Not only was I able to convert the entire dissertation into a variety of articles, many were reviewed by faculty members. In addition, I was able to develop a stronger application packet and compete in a much stronger manner. So although I had not considered this option, it helped change the trajectory of my career for the better.

• *Senior faculty.* You can often benefit from the wisdom, experience, and connections of senior faculty members. Full professors are typically well published and seasoned instructors and often provide excellent comments on academic articles. In addition, senior faculty may need graduate students to assist during research projects, to serve as teaching assistants, or to work on grant projects.

• *Junior faculty.* Graduate students may benefit from the recency of newer faculty members' knowledge and expertise. From their dissertation research, most junior faculty are abreast of the latest books, articles, and trends in the field. Having just recently been on the market and successfully located a position, they may have important, up-to-date suggestions for new candidates about employment trends and challenges they faced.

• *Other graduate students.* Graduate programs are hectic enough—no need to reinvent the wheel. Students can maximize their time by sharing information with each other, developing support groups, and providing feedback to each other. Interaction can and should occur across cohorts. During graduate school, a supportive professor helped me and a group of other students organize a teaching portfolio support group. Over a one year period, we worked with one another to develop and organize our teaching portfolios, critique each other's teaching statements, and review supporting documents. These teaching portfolios were ultimately central to locating employment. Working as a group works.

An additional suggestion about maximizing the graduate school experience is in order. Both the short- and long-term implications of your research and teaching interests should be considered, as well as where you are most interested in pursuing a position (i.e., at a research institution, teaching college, or institution that emphasizes both). It is important to pursue subjects that you feel passionate about and for which research and teaching will inform existing literature, students, and possibly the larger society. Note that views vary regarding how to focus your research and teaching interests. Some professors suggest the importance of having research and/or teaching exposure in a broad range of subject areas. This strategy makes for a more well-rounded scholar and instructor, and can broaden your marketability upon entering (or re-entering) the job market. Another camp suggests the need to specialize in a given subject area. Specificity in a given subject may be appropriate, but, if only two positions for faculty with such expertise are available, this may severely limit your academic job opportunities unless you have developed a profile that positions you competitively to teach and perform research in other areas as well. Based on your career goals, abilities, and interests, begin to think about how to position yourself early in graduate school and get advice from advisers and mentors.

■ The Importance of Publications and Publishing Strategies

Quite possibly the best way to gain a competitive advantage over many other candidates is to enter the job market with a publishing record. Typically this will set you apart from the pool of applicants more than any other credential. Publish or perish! This statement still holds true at many colleges and universities. And while the ability to teach effectively is also expected (refer to the section on the importance of teaching later in this chapter), academic publications are a powerful employment tool. Even candidates with articles under review are often considered more favorably than those without publications or without articles under review. Those without publications may find it difficult (but not impossible) to get interviews, especially at research-oriented institutions. Even institutions that focus on teaching are often more impressed by candidates who have begun a publishing agenda. Why is an initial publishing record so important? Well, it is important to show a search committee that you have already begun doing what most professors do—perform research and add to the literature in their discipline by publishing. Therefore, candidates who have established a publishing record or have begun to write for the academic arena are automatically more impressive and competitive. Although well-published academics make the process look easy, be mindful that getting a manuscript published requires a great deal of hard work, meticulous research and writing, and creativity—and the time and effort put into a manuscript does not guarantee its publication. Once a manuscript has been submitted, the process is out of your control. However, it is important to be proactive and intentional about those aspects of the process that you can influence.

Consider each paper, from a master's thesis to seminar papers, a potential publication. If given a choice of the type of paper to write in a course, it is best to choose a research paper rather than a traditional term paper (unless information from the term paper can be used in a literature review of a research paper). If possible, request course syllabi early to identify classes with a research and writing component. Take advantage of opportunities to collaborate on papers with faculty members (prepared with an idea and a type-written synopsis of the proposed project, seek out faculty members with whom to work). Not only can you hone your writing skills and learn how to develop and submit academic articles, but you can also pick up valuable writing and submission strategies from faculty members who have accomplished writing agendas. If given an opportunity to write a paper with a faculty member, be sure to maximize this experience. Ask questions about project framing, theoretical approaches, and methodological justification to gather information needed to spearhead your own publishing agenda in the future. A good goal should be to set aside time each week to work on papers for publication. If possible, begin this process no later than one year into graduate school. The time may be spent writing, editing, or reading other articles, but such efforts should focus on enhancing the manuscript on which you are working. Consider meeting with members of your cohort and organizing a writing support group. Whatever the strategy, it is important to establish consistent hours and days and try to maintain this schedule.

Consider the following factors when deciding where to submit a paper:

• *The paper's caliber.* Get an honest assessment from several faculty members. They can also suggest the most appropriate journal for the article.

• *Your point in graduate school.* Remember, it is important to have academic publications in peer-reviewed journals. Even if you are told that the paper has a good chance of serious consideration at a more competitive journal, a strategic decision should be made based on where you are in the graduate program. If you are relatively early in the program and the paper is deemed appropriate, it may be wise to submit the paper to a more competitive journal (i.e., the journal will have a low acceptance rate, but *if* the paper is accepted it would represent a major academic accomplishment). If you have not published and are nearing the end of your graduate program, it may be better to submit to a peer-reviewed journal with a somewhat higher acceptance rate to improve your chances of being selected. This is important because of the varied article review process (e.g., from 45 days for political science journals, three to nine months in sociology journals, and two years for some economics journals); a rejection means submitting to *another* journal and beginning the waiting process again. The best strategy will depend on your goals and the types of institutions to which you plan to apply. If you plan to apply for positions at institutions that require publications, then it is critical to get published. However, remember that certain institutions are more interested in candidates with publications in top journals in their discipline. Ask faculty members for advice about the best strategy for your current situation and employment goals.

How Many Publications Are Needed?

The best answer to this question is, unfortunately, it depends. If you are applying to teaching institutions, publications may not be as important as if you plan to apply to research institutions (although some teaching colleges are now more interested in candidates with publishing records). In addition, the expected number and caliber of publications will vary based on the type of research institution (for example, a Research I institution may tend to have more stringent publication requirements than a Research II institution or a teaching college). In general, it is best to have some type of publishing record when you enter the job market. If nothing else, it will allow you to have some flexibility. Without generalizing too much, given today's competitive market, the following rule is accepted—when applying for most positions, have at least one or two publications (preferably single-authored, but they can be co-authored) in peer-reviewed journals. In some instances, more is better. It is also impressive to have a few articles under review. This is an indication that a publishing pattern will continue after you are hired. However, this does not mean that candidates without publications should give up and not apply for positions for which they are qualified. If you wish to apply for a position, feel free to do so. Search committees consider factors other than publication records when making their decisions, but being aware of any "unstated" rules for successful competition will help you better prepare.

Getting published can be challenging, even under the best conditions. How can you improve your chances of achieving that goal? Here are a few strategies to consider:

• *Submit to an appropriate journal.* No matter how well researched and written your quantitatively-driven manuscript is, it will have little chance of being selected for publication if it is submitted to a journal that primarily publishes qualitative research. And a document focused on the history of health care may not be well-suited for a journal on postmodernist pedagogy. Be sure to research prospective journals and submit to those that have published work similar to your project. A review of journals may also uncover particular theoretical or political thrusts as well. Locate journals that provide the best fit for your submission and identify several options for possible resubmission in case your initial submission is rejected.

• *Review existing articles.* Read a variety of academic articles. Study their structure, style, and content. Note patterns and variations. Locate articles that are similar in format and focus to yours. Again, identify journals that tend to publish articles similar to your piece. This process will help you develop your article and make the best decision about where to submit. Once you become familiar with the academic writing process and publishing, volunteer to become a reviewer for a journal. Those experiences will help hone your writing skills, expose you to varied writing styles and research, and potentially help improve your writing ability.

• *Submit to "student-friendly" journals.* Faculty members are often aware of peer-reviewed journals that are more open to student submissions than others. Such journals may be interested in high-quality student papers to showcase. By focusing on such journals, you may increase the chances that your work will be accepted. However, note that most reviewers are not aware of the status (i.e., graduate student, assistant professor, full professor) of the writer of a submission, so focus on writing top quality papers for submission.

• *Submit to varied-tiered journals.* While it may be prestigious to publish in a "top-tiered" journal, in many cases the most important, short-term goal is to get published. The tier of certain journals is often assessed based on discipline history (i.e., flagship journals in the discipline), journal reputation, and, in some instances, impact factors. For example, certain impact factors (i.e., cites of recent articles divided by the number of recent articles) can be located in the ISI (Institute for Scientific Information) Journal Citation Reports®, Social Sciences Edition. Although debates continue to abound regarding how to determine journal rankings, their subjectivity, and value, you can make more informed publishing strategies if you know the relative ranking of the major journals in your discipline. Graduate directors and seasoned faculty members should have a list of the major journals in your discipline or can assist you in creating one. Use this list to develop submission strategies based on where you are in your graduate experience, as discussed previously. *Note:* Some academics may encourage students to only submit to top journals. However, this is a viable option to consider.

• *Consider a research note.* Due to their conciseness, shorter length (ten to fifteen pages), and possible ease of placement, some journals are more amendable to research notes. A research note may also serve as good practice for first-time writers before they progress to lengthier articles.

• *Consider a teaching/pedagogy journal.* It is quite common for graduate students to try innovative teaching techniques and creative methods to engage and instruct students. If you've developed an interesting teaching strategy or technology-based mode of instruction, document the process (and student evaluations, if available) and submit it to a teaching journal in your discipline.

• *Consider other publication options.* Book chapters, book reviews for publication (but not reviews for publishers), or possibly publishing a master's thesis as a monograph are other options to consider. Realize that the first two options are not comparable to an academic article, so be careful about spending too much time on such projects. However, if they can be completed expeditiously (for example, you are assigned to read a newly published book in a graduate seminar and spend a Saturday morning writing a review), they show your writing promise.

• *Try to obtain grants.* Most institutions offer a variety of internal grant opportunities. Also compete for national grants and grants through national and regional conferences. Even if a grant amount is minimal, acceptance is impressive because it shows that you are able to develop a proposal that is accepted and approved by a panel of scholars and that the proposal is worthy of funding.

• *Submit to newer journals.* Review national and regional conference bulletins for newly developed journals, special journal editions, and special book editions. These publishers may be open to nontraditional research and may also be more open to considering your submission.

• *Locate a reviewing mentor.* Identify several faculty members who are well published and available to read your work. Explain your publishing objectives to them and solicit their assistance. Because they are productive researchers and writers, they are probably quite busy, so be sure to inform them of the desired parameters of their involvement (i.e., time frames, review of documents to provide suggestions and comments for improvement). Give them at least one month to review your work and be sure to only provide them with your best writing. If you are respectful of their time and responsibilities and also show that you have promise as a researcher and writer, you are more apt to secure reviewing mentors.

Strategy: Setting Publication Limits

Although establishing a publishing record is important, it is wise to devise a publishing strategy. Yes, more is often better, but too many may be less than ideal. Using this strategy, you would set publication limits. This means you should attempt to have at least one publication upon graduation and several under review (or possibly in "forthcoming" or "revise and resubmit" stages). This will satisfy the publishing criteria for most institutions. Note that more prestigious or competitive institutions may only consider candidates with a variety of publications that are also in top journals. However, this appears to be the exception rather than the rule.

As a conscientious candidate, attempt to time several publications for release *after* you have begun your new tenure-track position. This will provide a "research cushion" to minimize the timing challenges associated with transitioning into a new academic position with all its responsibilities and also ensure that any accepted articles will count toward tenure. So it may *not* be ideal to publish a large number of articles before you accept a position, but rather to hold some of them until after you get a job and then submit them in your new position. However, articles that are accepted before you took a position, but that have yet to be published, can be credited toward your tenure record in your new position. There is generally a lag period between the time that an article is accepted and when it is published (usually several months). In order to get credit, contact the publisher as soon as you accept a position and make sure the job-granting institution's name and department (and not that of your graduate school) is referenced on the article. In doing so, you ensure that the article will be considered toward tenure. This is critical!

Although institutions usually consider current publications for candidate selection, these articles are often not *directly* considered toward tenure because the institution is not recognized in the publication. In many cases, new hires get full tenure credit for publications that occur *after* they accept a position. Thus it is important to publish while in graduate school and develop a publishing strategy while you are on the job market. Consider the above-mentioned strategy because it is often challenging to begin a new position, prepare for teaching responsibilities, and generate a variety of publications. A publishing strategy will help ease the transition into your new career.

Publishing Nitty-Gritty: How to Do It

This section includes a flowchart (Figure 3.1) and detailed comments to guide people in writing an academic article. Information is provided from conceptualizing to step-by-step points regarding each section of a manuscript. The flowchart focuses on research articles in the social sciences; however, understanding the process and key questions and issues at each step may prove beneficial to readers in other arenas. The flowchart also assumes you are using the standard academic format, and should be revised if the format in your discipline varies. If you are writing a largely qualitative article, some of the features and verbiage will change (i.e., linkages between dependent and independent variables, hypotheses, or even the use of such terms), but the overall process should be similar. Most important, the flowchart should be used to help you develop, process, and plan before you begin to write an article. Time spent conceptualizing and outlining the project will guide the entire endeavor and minimize wasted time associated with lack of organization. Also be sure to actually print out copies of each draft for review and edits. In this current age of computer technology some people may have become accustomed to only editing work online. I highly discourage this approach as the sole method for reviewing documents (whether they be manuscripts, cover letters, vitas, or even e-mails to a search committee chairperson). Although you may initially review a document online, always print a hardcopy and review it thoroughly by hand. This dual review process helps to ensure that you provide your best work. I also strongly recommend printing out and doing a hardcopy review of subsequent drafts after major revisions have been made.

In addition to the flowchart, certain issues should be considered before, during, and after an actual writing project. The following strategies should be considered no matter where you are in your academic writing career, but are key for the new graduate student, ABD, newly-minted Ph.D., or nontenured junior faculty

Figure 3.1 Academic Writing Flowchart

Abstract
(100–150 words)

The abstract should include at least four components:

- provide the research question/problem within the first two sentences
- describe the sample as well as methods used
- briefly state the main findings, being sure to tie them into the research question/problem
- end with an implication or conclusion based on the findings

Introduction
(1–2 pages)

In the introduction, be sure to:

- identify the research topic
- address why the topic is important (I refer to this as "the hook")
- identify the theory/framework
- explicitly state the research question(s)

In this section, identify the dependent variable(s) and key independent variables. Link and justify them. The dependent variable(s) refer to the topic of the research and the independent variables are explanatory indicators.

Tell the reader what you will be doing.

Literature review
(4–6 pages)

Summarize the books and articles related to the topic. Link them to the dependent and independent variables. Justify their inclusion.

(continues)

Theory
(2–3 pages)

Framework:
Summarize the study topic again and present hypotheses or expanded research questions. How is this study different? Link the discussion to the dependent variable(s), key independent variables, and past studies.

Logic Models:
To make things easier for the reader/reviewer, consider including a visual logic or conceptual model. They are very helpful to demonstrate hypothesized relationships among variables of interest. Therefore, they make it easier for readers to grasp the logic of the work. This can be rather easily done using the drawing menu in Microsoft Word. Again, doing so will help the researcher (and thus the reader) think more clearly and succinctly about this work's theoretical model.

Some helpful examples and instructions can be found at *http://www.wkkf.org/Pubs/Tools/Evaluation/Pub3669.pdf* and *http://www.cdc.gov/search.do?action=search&queryText=logic+model*.

Key Transition Paragraph:
The paragraph immediately before the methods section is an extremely important one. In it, the author should
• remind the reader of the research question
• again, briefly state the limitations of previous research in addressing the question/problem
• while referring to his or her own methodology, briefly tell the reader how this research will fill that gap

(continues)

(Figure 3.1 continued)

This paragraph serves as a cognitive roadmap to remind the reader what the author is doing and what to expect from the paper.

Data and methods
(3–4 pages)

When writing the methods section, the author should keep two things in mind—specify and justify. The author should specify exactly what she or he is doing and what data and methods will be employed; while doing so, justify exactly why that sample and methodology were chosen.

Describe data and variables. Identify limitations.

In a reader-friendly fashion, describe and justify methods.

Organize/present the information in a logical format.

Findings
(3–4 pages)

Present findings and any atypical results.

Don't forget to use a reader-friendly approach and to organize/present the information in a logical format.

Tell the reader what you are doing.

Discussion/conclusion
(4–6 pages)

Discussion:
In this section of the paper (and not in this particular order):

• briefly summarize the important results
• inform the reader of what these results mean and their larger implication
• tie the results back to the literature,

(Figure 3.1 continued)

theories, and/or hypotheses discussed in the background/literature review (supported/refuted)
• discuss the limitations of the research
• make it even more clear how the research/findings contribute to the field (this could include policy implications)
• delineate areas for future research

Don't make the mistake of simply duplicating the findings section. Instead, pick out two or three important findings, highlight them, and then spend time developing each. Are there any theories that are particularly supported or refuted given these findings? Tie these findings back to the literature discussed earlier in the paper. If there is no such literature currently in the paper, add it, and then link it here.

It's in this section where the author's scholarly imagination should shine brightest. Here the author should showcase her/himself as not just a consumer of knowledge, but a producer of one, an innovative thinker.

Conclusion:
End the paper on a strong note. Consider restating the research problem, and offering, in light of this research, a succinct answer to the research question/problem. Most important, end strongly!

Tell the reader what you told them.

References, Tables, Endnotes

member. Unlike the strategies presented earlier in this section, these comments are more applied and directly related to completing the finished product—an academic manuscript for submission.

• *Mine the data.* Whether your data are numbers or words, be sure to maximize their use. Although the number will vary based on the type and amount of data available, you should plan to write at least three articles per data file at your disposal. If you have only developed an idea for one article based on your current data, expand your thought processes (some suggestions are provided below). A conversation with the members of your dissertation committee may also stimulate your imagination about possible ways in which the dissertation data can be published.

• *Perform a theory test.* Some of the strongest publications have been tests of traditional theories using current data. Can you test a theory developed during the Industrial Revolution on contemporary US experiences? Will your data enable you to test a dimension of rational choice theory? This approach can be used to put a creative spin on traditional academic information. If you do not perform a theory test, be sure your manuscript is grounded in a theory or theoretical framework.

• *Don't discount "old" data.* Some people avoid analyzing data that are considered too old (for example, over ten years since they were collected). However, based on your research subject, the age of the data may not be a major issue. If you can justify why use of the data overshadows its age, this approach may enable you to gain access to a database to be mined (because you are more apt to find existing publications based on older data, they may also provide you with ideas about how to creatively use the data to add to the current literature in your discipline).

• *Take a short course.* Courses of varied length (for example, one day, one week, and four weeks) are available during the summer months that can be helpful for acquiring additional skills in order to publish, stimulating ideas for research projects, and interacting with graduate student peers. For example, a variety of courses are offered through the Interuniversity Consortium for Political and Social Research (ICPSR) that are germane to people in the social sciences and, in some instances, the humanities.

• *Creatively consider research options.* It is important to "think outside the box" when developing research ideas. It is possible to put a new spin on an existing subject that will result in an innovative research topic. Consider studying the attitudes and behavior of respondents for comparative purposes; performing intergroup tests based on factors such as race, sex, class, and sexual orientation; or replicating an existing study based on a different group (for example, take a previous study based on white respondents and examine the subject based on the experiences of Asians). Attempt to imagine topics in your discipline that would attract reviewers and readers or "hot" topics that are of interest to you. Identify a limitation in the current literature and perform research that attempts to address it.

• *Determine the "hook."* The hook refers to that feature (or features) of your research that is unique or different, that makes the research worthy of publication. The hook may be a unique data set or cutting-edge methods, a void in the current literature, a direct theory test that has yet to be performed, or an analysis of an under-examined topic or group of people. An exciting, innovative hook can be the difference between a mediocre manuscript and one worthy of immediate consideration.

• *Do not forget the importance of a well-written manuscript.* No matter how impressive the research idea or the data, nothing will compensate for a poorly written document. In general, the document should answer who, what, where, when, why, and how. Be sure to write well (edit your work, use spell check, follow submission guidelines, and use the appropriate format). Justify each section of the article—explain why each section is important. Describe why you are performing the particular study. What are the limitations in each section (especially data and methods)? Be sure the literature review is complete. Rather than being an annotated bibliography, the literature review should frame the project and establish the importance of the research question(s). Cited research should summarize existing conceptual and empirical work and synthesize the material into a coherent argument that justifies the research question. Write using simple, clear research questions and, if appropriate, propositions and hypotheses. Avoid unduly long sentences and an overly long manuscript.

Keep the analysis simple and based on the smallest unit of analysis and the most appropriate methods for the research question and data. The manuscript should be tightly written and reflect your best work.

• *Follow model papers and the discipline process.* One of the best ways to master academic writing is to follow the format of model papers. Locate publications that are considered stellar in your discipline or subfield and closely examine the writing style and format. Use such articles as templates for your writing. And avoid taking short cuts when writing and performing research. Such decisions may initially seem to expedite the process, but they usually only lengthen it in terms of edits, mistakes, and poorly organized work.

Write, write, write. I was reminded that the Latino novelist Rudolfo Anaya once noted that two things are necessary to make a living by writing. You have to have something to say and you have to make it interesting. Most academics earn a living writing; practice will hone this skill.

Writing a Book

Although the previous section on publishing focuses on developing academic articles, a few comments are necessary regarding book publishing. I focus on the article-writing process because, in most instances, graduate students, ABDs, and junior faculty are encouraged to publish articles initially and to consider writing a book post-tenure. However, in disciplines such as history and certain foreign languages, having a book project underway is crucial in order to locate a tenure-track position and a published book is mandatory to be competitive for tenure. If you are in a discipline for which this is the case, you may be advised to focus your attention during graduate school on writing the dissertation—with the intention to convert it into a monograph upon graduation. However, you may be encouraged to publish a few academic papers along with the plan to convert the dissertation into a book. It is important to converse with your graduate director, adviser, and mentors about whether you should begin to write a book and, if so, the appropriate timing and logistics surrounding the process.

I do not focus on book projects here because, again, they seem to be generally more important once a candidate has located a tenure-track position.

◼ The Importance of Teaching

Even the most research-oriented institutions may require teaching skills of new faculty. Since many schools provide graduate students with opportunities as teaching assistants or instructors, take advantage of these experiences and develop teaching strategies that will benefit you on the job market. Thus it is important to get as much teaching experience as possible. Develop a teaching strategy that reflects depth as well as breadth. If possible, given specific departmental constraints and needs, try to teach in your areas of focus. In addition, attempt to teach several different types of courses (keep in mind that new course preparations will slow down your dissertation completion). These courses, listed on the vita and in the teaching portfolio, show your strengths and experiences in classroom settings.

Developing and teaching new courses also shows initiative and creativity. Each course should be evaluated by students, peers, and/or faculty members. This documentation is typically requested during the application process. Some institutions may severely limit graduate teaching; others do not allow graduate students to teach courses at all. If departmental restrictions exist, it may still be worthwhile for more senior graduate students to request to teach their own course. This shows responsibility, a willingness to accept new challenges, and the desire to take on the role of professor. However, before accepting such a role, make sure you are comfortable and prepared because it will be important to receive good evaluations. If possible, seek opportunities to teach in other academic settings. This may mean serving as an adjunct professor at a local two-year institution, community college, or technical school, or making numerous conference presentations. These teaching episodes can be listed on your vita and represent credible experience in the classroom.

■ Presenting at Conferences and Meetings

Speaking at conferences is possibly one of the easiest, most beneficial methods for preparing for interviews and getting "teaching" experience. Most conferences welcome student participation. Most even have student-sponsored sessions. Local and regional conferences are especially open to student involvement. Because departments realize the student-friendly nature of most conferences and meetings, they often provide departmental support for travel and expenses. Benefits of conference participation include:

• *Networking.* These settings provide an opportunity to share information with others about your research interests and possibly establish relationships with collaborators for future research projects. Other attendees and faculty members may be aware of employment openings as well.

• *Developing presentation skills.* Conference speaking enables students to develop critical presentation skills that will be needed when interviewing. These include the ability to concisely summarize information within specific time constraints, answer random questions ad lib, and speak extemporaneously. Be sure to meet deadlines for submitting abstracts and/or papers to panel organizers and participants and for posting the paper to a conference. This will help establish a reputation as a professional.

• *Developing social skills.* Conference meetings often involve socializing with other academics. You can learn skills regarding social etiquette and interacting in informal group settings. These skills will be important during lunch and dinner interviews, impromptu gatherings onsite, and more casual settings during onsite interviews.

• *Gaining insight into teaching.* Because preparing to speak at a conference is similar to preparing to teach a class, this can be good practice. Conference involvement is especially crucial if you have limited teaching opportunities in your graduate program.

• *Practicing.* Just as it will be important to prepare and practice before formal job interviews, practice for conference speaking engagements. This type of preparation will establish the foundation for the type of structured, formal practice needed for a formal interview. In addition, a well-prepared presentation may impress faculty members in the audience who may take note of you for a current or future employment position.

• *Participating in paper competitions.* Compete in as many conference-sponsored paper competitions as possible. Benefits may include a monetary reward, recognition, and the opportunity to present your work during a conference-wide session. In addition, such honors make an impressive addition to your vita.

• *Attending job fairs.* Many national conferences sponsor employment or job fairs where students can interview for available positions. Such interviews can be practice opportunities for more formal interviews to come as well as places to put out job "feelers." Roundtable participation can also help hone speaking skills.

▓ Job Market Preparation Timeline

This section includes suggestions for linking each phase of your graduate career to your subsequent attempt to locate an academic position. This means preparing to enter the job market from the time you enter graduate school until program completion. The goal is to maximize the graduate school experience. You are encouraged to develop and follow a timeline similar to the example included in this section (Figure 3.2). The timeline provides a step-by-step set of milestones that can be used to develop and organize the important components of your application packet: the vita, teaching portfolio, publications, teaching experience, and service. By creating a process, you will be better able to incorporate these components into your graduate studies and consider them when making decisions during graduate school. The importance of starting and maintaining a timeline cannot be overemphasized. Setting and meeting small milestones along the way will lessen the need for major preparations at the end of graduate school.

You may question your ability to prepare to enter the job market while simultaneously earning a Ph.D. Establishing a job market timeline will place each phase of your graduate career within the context of preparing for the job market. This means that each course, each departmental requirement, and each opportunity for research, teaching, and service becomes purposed and linked together. Thus you will be more apt to make informed decisions and associate your choices to both your academic goal (earning a Ph.D.) and subsequent professional goal (locating academic employment).

The timeline below assumes you have a master's degree and are entering a five-year graduate program. Your timeline will change based on how long it takes to complete each phase of graduate school (i.e., coursework, comprehensive exams, oral exams, specialty projects, data collection, data analyses, and dissertation). For example, expect the timeline to expand considerably, possibly by two to three years after coursework completion and dissertation project approval, if you plan to collect and transcribe your own data. Revise it accordingly. The timeline is also based on the graduate student who enters school in the fall semester of a given year and plans to graduate at the end of the spring semester of year five. Revise your timeline if your graduate program is longer or shorter or if major life events result in changes in your graduate work.

The first two years of the program (and the timeline) are crucial. During this period in most graduate programs, you are focused primarily on completing coursework. Because of this structure, you will be better able to develop a timeline and adhere to it before you become focused on collecting data and/or completing the dissertation during your final years. Once you have established the structure of your timeline, review it periodically (every three to four months) and update it with your teaching, research, and/or service accomplishments. Establish a routine. This can easily be done by placing letters, accomplishments, honors, and references to other academic achievements in an accordion file. Each time you review, simply remove the contents included during that period and update your application packet. Although you should feel comfortable revising your timeline, it is important to maintain a schedule that allows you to progress toward your ultimate goals of successfully completing the dissertation in a timely fashion and preparing to be a competitive employment candidate. If you are already underway in a graduate program (i.e., this is your second year), revise the timeline to reflect the different time period (you may also have to catch up relative to certain milestones).

The timeline is arranged to result in the following: a vita, a teaching portfolio, two academic publications, four presentations, and one grant. And while you have no control over certain aspects of this process (e.g., whether a journal accepts your submission or a conference organizer selects your presentation proposal), you will be able to proactively establish milestones and prepare to enter the job market. The timeline should be used as a guide. Feel free to establish higher standards, such as doubling up on publishing or teaching another course, but not at the expense of graduate school requirements needed to earn your Ph.D. Note that the timeline does not include information about a specific graduate program, but rather guidelines related to preparing for a job search. Components of the timeline are addressed in more detail in other chapters of this book.

* * *

Figure 3.2 Sample Timeline

Year 1 (fall)

❑ Think about your area(s) of focus or topics of interest.
❑ Develop a draft of your vita.
❑ Start or join a teaching portfolio support group (recruit cohort members and other interested graduate students).
❑ Begin a teaching portfolio (compile major accomplishments, honors from your master's program, and special honors from undergraduate school [e.g., Phi Beta Kappa]).
❑ Submit a proposal from your master's thesis to present at a regional conference.
❑ Discuss academic plans with the graduate director.
❑ Begin to look for an adviser among faculty members.
❑ Try to get a teaching assistantship (TA) or graduate research assistantship (RA) position (if you don't have a post via a graduate fellowship).

Year 1 (spring)

❑ Determine your area(s) of focus or topics of interest.
❑ Think about potential dissertation topics of interest.
❑ Update your vita.
❑ Decide on a publication project (a portion of the master's thesis or an article or research note from a writing assignment from a fall course). Paper #1.
❑ Ask several faculty members to review the draft of paper #1 (possibly the professor for whose course you initially wrote the paper). Complete the paper during summer.
❑ Update your teaching portfolio (add student evaluations if you taught during fall, year 1).
❑ Ask a faculty member to be your mentor (some may be unavailable due to their schedules, so have several potential candidates).
❑ Meet with the teaching portfolio support group.
❑ Present at a regional conference (begin to prepare late fall, year 1).

Year 1 (summer)

❑ Complete paper #1.

(continues)

Year 2 (fall)

- ❑ Submit paper #1.
- ❑ Select a paper from a spring year 1 course to submit to a regional or national conference.
- ❑ Update your vita.
- ❑ Find a faculty member to co-author a paper with (ask a professor from a class you took where you did well; consider using the research paper from that course as the basis for the paper). Paper #2.
- ❑ Update teaching portfolio (if teaching, ask a faculty member known for his/her teaching to observe one of your teaching sessions and write a letter of evaluation).
- ❑ Update teaching portfolio (include summaries from your student evaluations).
- ❑ Meet with the teaching portfolio support group.
- ❑ Meet with mentor.
- ❑ Ask graduate director and search Internet for grants in your area.
- ❑ Prepare for paper presentation at regional conference, if applicable.

Year 2 (spring)

- ❑ Make changes to paper #1. Revise and resubmit; if rejected, incorporate revisions based on reviewer comments and ask a faculty member to review the revised document. Submit to another journal.
- ❑ Continue to work on paper #2 (co-authored paper with professor). Complete paper in summer, year 2.
- ❑ Meet with the teaching portfolio support group.
- ❑ Apply for a grant.
- ❑ Speak at a regional conference, if applicable.
- ❑ Meet with mentor.
- ❑ Update teaching portfolio (if teaching, ask a junior faculty member to observe one of your teaching sessions and write a letter of evaluation).

Year 2 (summer)

- ❑ Complete paper #2.
- ❑ Prepare for paper presentation at national conference, if applicable.

(continues)

(Figure 3.2 continued)

Year 3 (fall)

❏ Update your vita.
❏ Update your teaching portfolio (include student evaluations).
❏ Present during national conference, if applicable.
❏ Submit paper #2 (paper co-authored with professor).
❏ Determine faculty references.
❏ Submit paper for conference (try a national conference if you have not done so).
❏ Meet with the teaching portfolio support group.
❏ Meet with mentor.
❏ Continue to teach.
❏ Prepare for paper presentation at regional conference, if applicable.

Year 3 (spring)

❏ Make changes to paper #2. Revise and resubmit; if rejected, incorporate revisions based on reviewer comments and ask a faculty member to review the revised document. Submit to another journal.
❏ Update vita.
❏ Meet with the teaching portfolio support group.
❏ Update teaching portfolio.
❏ Meet with mentor.
❏ Present at a regional conference.

Year 3 (summer)

❏ Prepare for paper presentation at national conference, if applicable.

Year 4 (fall)

❏ Update vita.
❏ Interview at national conference (as ABD); present paper, if applicable.
❏ Meet with the teaching portfolio support group.
❏ Meet with mentor.
❏ If they have not been accepted, make decisions about papers #1 and

(Figure 3.2 continued)

#2 (this includes making major revisions and letting well-published faculty members provide suggestions such as whether to convert to research notes or hold and focus on dissertation).

❑ Update teaching portfolio (if teaching, ask senior faculty member or department head to observe one of your teaching sessions and write a letter of evaluation).

Year 4 (spring)

❑ Begin to prepare "job talk" (use dissertation as a foundation).
❑ Begin formally compiling parts of your application packet.
❑ Update vita.
❑ Update teaching portfolio.
❑ Meet with mentor.
❑ Meet with the teaching portfolio support group.

Year 5 (fall)

❑ Enter job market for possible position in fall following graduation.
❑ Interview at national conference.
❑ Update vita and teaching portfolio (create final versions).
❑ Bring together your application packet materials.
❑ Meet with the teaching portfolio support group.
❑ Meet with mentor.

Year 5 (spring)

❑ Continue to interview, if necessary, for possible position in fall following graduation.
❑ Make periodic updates of vita and teaching portfolio.
❑ Meet with the teaching portfolio support group.
❑ Meet with mentor.
❑ Graduate and prepare to relocate to new position.

4

The Application Process

This chapter focuses on important topics to consider as you develop application strategies and begin to apply for positions. The application process can be extremely demanding. In addition to applying for positions, most candidates are also completing graduate school requirements and teaching. To make the process easier and more efficient, it is best to have an organized plan. Some thought should go into this plan and associated strategies. Important questions to consider include: Where to apply? How to apply? How to best present yourself? Who to ask for letters of reference? What timing considerations should be made? After these types of questions are answered and an application structure is in place, it should be followed methodically. This will help ensure that the correct documents are sent to the appropriate institutions within the allotted time period. It also makes it quicker and easier to track submissions and the status of supporting documents provided by others. As noted earlier, organizational skills are crucial. Once certain documents have been reviewed and completed (e.g., vita, writing samples, teaching portfolio), ten to fifteen copies of each should be kept in separate folders so that they can easily be located for a particular job advertisement. It will be necessary to revise and print or obtain certain documents for each application packet (e.g., cover letters and letters of reference). Remember, search committees may review hundreds of application packets for a single position; the goal is to develop an application packet that stands out for positive reasons.

■ Pre-Application Considerations

Before beginning the application process, think about what types of positions interest you, because this will affect the focus of the search. Are you interested in positions at teaching colleges? Research institutions? Research I institutions? Would you prefer a large public institution or small private one? Would life in a city be preferable to a rural community? Is working at a prestigious institution or well-known department most important? Is there a preference for a certain region of the country? Or are you more flexible in terms of the type of institution, region, size, and prestige level? Are there spousal, partner, or parental considerations to be made? Although it will not be easy to locate a position that meets all your preferences (e.g., location), these types of issues should be raised before you begin to apply because they will affect where you apply. Once these questions have been answered, begin to scan employment bulletins and the Internet and discuss options with faculty members to select the schools to which you will apply. For example, if relocation is not an option, then schools outside the immediate area should not be considered. By the same token, if you are only interested in working at a teaching institution, you probably should not apply for positions at research institutions (some students may experience pressure from advisers to only apply and accept positions from higher-status institutions). One word of caution, unless there are specific reasons that prevent you from applying to a variety of institutions (e.g., a partner or spouse with a great career that prevents relocation), it may be best to be flexible in the application process. This brings us to the next important issue—the appropriate number of places to which you should apply.

Several viewpoints are appropriate relative to this issue. In general, be selective. For example, although the University of Granada may advertise a position that seems *perfect,* it is illogical to apply if you are not remotely interested in living there. However, also apply to as many institutions as possible that are searching for candidates with your credentials. Given that the job market is competitive, it is best to spread a selective net to increase your options (for example, at least twenty-five appropriate institutions, but you must decide the breadth of your net).

Candidates also often ask, "Should I apply to prestigious institutions that offer positions in my area?" Again, there is no correct answer. Some professors suggest that, given the level of competition and the tendency for many prestigious institutions to severely restrict their pool of applicants, candidates who have not attended similarly ranked institutions have little chance for consideration. This is probably the case. However, use your own discretion to make this decision (remember, this is your career, so it should be your decision). If you are really interested in a position, then applying is not out of the question. And if you are not accepted, all that has been lost is some time and effort. If, however, the institution is interested, there may be the possibility for an interview and subsequent job offer. Early in your graduate career, it will also be important to gather information about the supply and demand for people in your intended area(s) of specialization. This information should inform decisions made during graduate school as well as during the application process.

The next section addresses how to follow instructions in advertisements and specific points to note when reviewing ads. The profile of a typical search committee and their considerations and concerns as they evaluate a pool of candidates are also discussed. Next, pointers are provided to develop an application packet as well as application strategies. The chapter also includes guidelines to develop a cover letter and vita based on whether you are applying to a research or teaching institution. Lastly, a sample application schedule is included that can be used to log and track applications.

■ Advertisements: Following Instructions and Reading Between the Lines

Positions are usually advertised in academic employment bulletins, online services, employment brochures and magazines, and printed fliers distributed by institutions (refer to discipline-specific outlets as well as *The Chronicle of Higher Education*). Specific submission requirements are provided in the ads. The first hurdle used to weed out candidates may be whether or not they follow the application instructions. This section contains four examples of employment notices that have been dissected to point out some of their most important features. Advertisements vary in form and content, but usually include the following components:

- Position title and level (tenure-track, nontenure track, 2-year renewable contract, assistant professor, associate professor, full professor, program director)
- Areas of focus and any required specializations
- Department(s) spearheading the search
- Required education (Ph.D. in hand, ABD) and skills for the position (existing research record, potential for research, teaching experience)
- Date position begins
- Requirements of selected candidate (research, teach, develop seminars, service activities)
- Demographic information about the institution and the surrounding area
- Documents required from the applicant (cover letter, vita, teaching portfolio, letters of reference, transcripts)
- Deadline (postmarked by, received by)
- Name of the contact person or a generic contact (chair of search committee, Dr. Jane Jones).

It is important to identify these parts in each job posting. As you review the following four examples of job postings (Figures 4.1–4.4), your goal is to determine the application requirements and the *stated* as well as important *implied* aspects of the position. In each case, I provide comments in terms of the job's implications. Note that some of the examples have points in common.

An important part of the initial application process is learning how to "read and respond" to job postings. Although you may be tempted to mass mail your application material to a variety of institutions, be careful. It is more important to decide whether the position represents a match between the requirements and your skills and interests. As mentioned earlier, part of the initial screening process is identifying candidates who do not follow directions as provided in the advertisement. So while it is important to stand out from the candidate pool, be sure to provide the material

Figure 4.1 The Teaching College

Advertisements from teaching institutions will stress the importance of teaching and mentoring students as well as evidence of effective teaching.

The Department of Ethnic International Studies invites applicants for three tenure-track assistant professorships in cultural or postcolonial studies. For two of the three positions, we are seeking candidates whose research and teaching competencies are primarily focused on Latino populations in the US, while the third position is open. The effective date is January 1, 2006. Specializations in political economy and gender are especially desirable. Earned Ph.D. required prior to appointment. Appointee expected to teach (3–4 teaching load), develop new courses, and mentor students. Research and publications are expected, as are service contributions.

Scanland College is an attractive, small undergraduate teaching institution in Sandy Springs, Georgia, with easy access to Atlanta. The town offers good public schools and a quiet, picturesque environment. Applicants should send a cover letter, curriculum vita, a teaching portfolio that includes student evaluations, three current and original letters of reference, and a writing sample postmarked by October 10 to:

> Chair, Search Committee
> Ethnic International Studies Department
> 227 South Hall
> Scanland College
> Sandy Springs, Georgia 00000

Transcript showing highest degree will be required of final candidates. Scanland College is an Affirmative Action and Equal Opportunity employer and encourages applications from women, minorities, veterans, and people with disabilities.

- Teaching colleges tend to stress teaching over research. Candidates who are more interested in research than teaching should note this.
- Three tenure-track positions are available. This provides more options for candidates.
- Only assistant professor positions are available.
- Unlike most, these positions would begin mid-academic year. Consider this in terms of possible graduation dates and other responsibilities.

(continues)

(Figure 4.1 continued)

- Although specializations are noted, they are general enough that a wide variety of areas might be appropriate.
- Candidates must have a Ph.D. before they are accepted for the position. In such instances, conditional acceptance is possible. However, some institutions will not consider a candidate unless she/he has "Ph.D. in hand."
- Note the teaching load (three to four courses). This is typically the case for teaching institutions. Research is often expected as well, but to a lesser degree. Student mentoring and service are typically very important. Be mindful that heavier teaching loads and mentoring responsibilities may make it difficult for you to find time to take part in consistent research.
- The college is located in a small town with access to a large city.
- Extensive documentation is required. Many of the application requirements could be addressed with a teaching portfolio.
- The application packet is acceptable if postmarked by the deadline date. This gives candidates additional time to complete the packet.
- School only has undergraduate students. This may be a concern for some candidates. Graduate programs provide faculty with advanced students for research and teaching purposes. Some candidates may only wish to apply to departments with both undergraduate and graduate students.

Figure 4.2 The Summarized Posting

This type of advertisement reflects institutions that market in employ-ment bulletins with space constraints or in electronically submitted advertisements.

> The Department of Political Science at Banks University invites appli-cations in political theory, including scholars with expertise in the pol-itics of culture and diasporic politics (lecturer with the potential to transition into a tenure-track Assistant Professor's position or tenured Associate), effective July 1, 2007. Applicants must have a Ph.D. and exhibit a high potential for excellence in research and teaching at both the undergraduate and graduate levels. Vita, evidence of teaching quality, copies of research papers, separate statement of teaching phi-losophy, and names and e-mail addresses of three references will be accepted through the postmark of November 15, 2006, and should be addressed to: Professor Peter Taylor, Search Committee Chair, Dept. of Political Science, 330 Brown Hall, Banks University, San Francisco, CA 00000. Banks University is an Equal Opportunity employer.

- Several types of positions are available (tenured and nontenured).
- New graduates should note that a tenure-track assistant professor posi-tion is not available. Some candidates may be leery of applying for the lecturer position because it is not tenure-track.
- The statement "high potential for excellence in research and teaching" may suggest an institution with a rigorous research agenda and diffi-cult tenure-granting process (this is important for those considering the lecturer position). Also ask senior faculty members about the insti-tution's reputation.
- Teaching documents are required (you can simply provide a teaching portfolio).
- E-mail addresses of references are requested. The search committee will most likely contact references directly.
- Application must be postmarked by a specific date (not arrive by). This will give candidates more time to apply.

Figure 4.3 The Bulleted Posting

This type of advertisement is often circulated via a wide canvass to a variety of institutions for posting. Such institutions are quite specific in their requirements and present the posting in a manner that is reader friendly.

PLEASE POST
Department of Mathematics
Announcement of Opening

Position: Tenure-track position, Assistant Professor, Mathematics with specialization in Complex Numbers

Effective Date: September 1, 2007

Minimum Qualifications:
- Ph.D. (at time of appointment) in Mathematics or related science or in an area with a graduate focus on Complex numbers from an accredited university
- Potential for successful college level teaching
- Ability to communicate with an ethnically and culturally diverse campus community
- Potential for continuing development of research programs

Desired/Preferred Qualifications:
- Academic expertise in the area of Complex numbers or integer analysis
- Evidence of scholarship and successful teaching in one or more of the following: Complex Numbers, Theory, Real Analysis, and Integral Analysis
- Ability to mentor students
- Ability to develop courses for international students in above areas
- Evidence of community and campus service

Duties:
- Teach undergraduate Complex numbers course and graduate courses as needed by the department
- Develop courses in areas of focus
- Engage in scholarly and creative activity
- Participate in program, university, and community service
- Assist in mentoring students
- Assist the department, college, and campus in developing curriculum, pedagogies, and programs to meet the needs of a diverse student body

(continues)

(Figure 4.3 continued)

Salary Range:
Commensurate with training and experience. Probable range is $45,000 to $49,000.

Required Documentation:
Letter of application addressing minimal and desired/preferred qualifications and stating research and teaching interests; vita; three letters of reference; teaching evaluations; brief statements of teaching and research interests; and official transcript from each institution attended. Employment is contingent upon proof of the legal right to work in the US. ABDs considered, but must have Ph.D. by appointment. Documents must reach us by December 20, 2006. Position will remain open until appropriate candidate is found. Mail applications to: Professor Sandra Bobler, Dept. of Mathematics, 222 Smith St., Science University, Indianapolis, IN 00000.

- Diverse campus (candidate must be able to effectively work with people from different backgrounds).
- Student mentoring is noted in several places (candidate should decide if they wish to have such responsibilities).
- Community and university involvement as well as research and teaching are required.
- Salary is noted (candidate can immediately decide if the range is acceptable and warrants application).
- The required teaching evaluations and brief statements of teaching and research interests can be addressed in a teaching portfolio. Also, the posting requires a variety of supporting documents. This process may automatically weed out less conscientious candidates (candidates should also allow sufficient time to collect the required application documents).

Figure 4.4 The General Advertisement

Advertisement suggests the broad needs of the department. A slightly vague advertisement can foster a large application pool.

The University of Miami–Central announces a multidisciplinary search for a tenure-track Assistant Professor to begin Fall 2007 with research specialties in demography or topics related to demography. Applications are invited from scholars whose primary academic appointment would be in one of the following departments: Anthropology, Geography and Planning, or Sociology. The successful candidate will also play an active role in the University's Center for Urban and Demographic Analysis. Preference will be given to candidates with research programs in migration, population distribution, and urban demography, but strong candidates with other research interests will also be considered.

In addition to having a Ph.D. at the time of appointment, candidates should demonstrate the potential for excellence in research, attract external funding (especially from NSF and NIH), and exhibit a strong commitment to teaching and service. Applications will be screened beginning December 1, 2006. Applicants should send a letter of interest, curriculum vita, and three letters of reference to: Demography Search Committee, Center for Urban and Demographic Analysis, University of Miami–Central, 1500 Smith Ave., Miami, Florida 00000. Other materials will be requested if needed. This position is contingent upon final budgetary approval. The University of Miami–Central is an equal opportunity/affirmative action/IRCA/ADA employer.

- Committee will consider candidates from varied disciplines (posting is somewhat vague and broad in terms of the areas of focus for an appropriate candidate).
- Role with University's Center for Urban and Demographic Analysis opens possibilities for publishing relationships, creative projects, grant writing, and administrative responsibilities.
- The ability to acquire external funding is noted (from extremely competitive sources); this suggests a potentially rigorous research environment.
- Teaching and service are still required (another possible level of rigor to note).

(continues)

(Figure 4.4 continued)

- Note "screening" date. Again, a vague deadline (candidates should do their best to make sure application materials reach the committee before the date. However, given the vague deadline, interested candidates who learn of the advertisement late should also apply).

- Candidates should expect to be contacted for additional supporting documents. Contact will also let you know the institution is considering you for the position.

- The position has not been finalized. This is important because you should realize that the position may be canceled or delayed indefinitely due to budgetary issues. The point here is to apply to a variety of institutions.

requested in the job posting and carefully read each posting to determine whether you are really interested in or a fit for the position. Reading between the lines requires you to accurately dissect the important features of each job posting and consider them with respect to your professional and personal goals and objectives. If you are unsure about the content of a job posting, seek the advice of a member of your graduate program and also feel free to contact the institution directly for clarification.

The Search Committee

As its name suggests, the search committee spearheads the departmental search for acceptable candidates to fill a position or positions. This group acts on behalf of the department or program and streamlines the decisionmaking process. In medium- to large-sized departments, the committee typically includes three to seven faculty members who represent a cross section of the department members. Full professors, associate professors, assistant professors, and, in some instances, a graduate student representative, may be asked to serve as members at any given time. At many smaller institutions with small departments, the search committee may consist of one or two departmental faculty as well as faculty members from other departments or disciplines. Regardless of departmental size, noncommittee members in the interested department are able to review applicant files, but the search committee is typically given responsibility to select candidates. Such committees are often also responsible to the university dean, assistant dean, or another administrator. And at smaller institutions, the provost and president may be involved in the interview and selection process. Because of a potentially large applicant pool, a great deal of time and energy is spent determining acceptable candidates. Committees typically begin the initial search process in the fall of an academic year to fill a position by the fall of the following year. Goals often include: expanding an existing department or departmental program by adding faculty, enhancing a current departmental focus, adding staff to a newly developed area of focus, or replacing retiring, retired, or deceased faculty.

Search Committee Lists

The search committee's task is to select a group of potential candidates from a large pool of applicants. This process usually occurs in stages. During the first stage, all applicants are considered. This requires the committee to review all application packets. During a series of meetings, committee members discuss the applicants, eliminate candidates who are obviously ill-fitted for the position (refer to the "ideal candidate" below), and attempt to reduce the pool to a more manageable group of applicants. Often referred to as a "long" or a "long-short" list, this group of ten to fifteen candidates is then reviewed in more detail. In some cases, telephone interviews may be conducted and additional supporting documents may be requested in order to reduce this group of applicants. The final "short" list usually consists of three to four candidates who are offered onsite interviews. Because people who make the short list may have already accepted positions elsewhere or decide to decline an interview, the search committee may have several alternates. However, some openings are so specific that few candidates apply. This does not exempt a search committee from rigorously reviewing the applicants. Nor does it mean that those few applicants will automatically receive interviews. It is not uncommon to extend an application deadline or to end a search due to a lack of appropriate or qualified candidates.

The "Ideal Candidate"

Who is the search committee looking for? What are some of the characteristics of the so-called ideal candidate? Of course, there is no ideal candidate, but, theoretically, the committee has such a candidate in mind and they consider the following types of issues:

- *An academic fit.* First and foremost, a candidate must have credentials that parallel the requirements for the position. This typically means that the candidate must possess expertise, course-work, and training in the desired areas of study as well as a teaching and/or publication record (or potential in these areas). Some search committees may have a broad set of requirements, but most are looking for a specific set of skills. It goes without saying that if Blakely University wishes to hire a political scientist with expertise in econometrics and you have never even *heard* of econometrics, then you are probably not a good academic fit. However, if the institution will consider people with a wide array of interests, it may be worthwhile to apply. Carefully review the advertisement to determine whether your areas of interest correspond or are in some way related to those desired by the institution. Doing so will save you and a search committee a great deal of time and effort because in most cases, no matter how stellar you are as a candidate, if your academic focus is not needed, you will probably not be considered for the position (however, refer to the section More About Academic Spousal Hiring in Chapter 8). This type of decision is made early in the search process to determine the small pool of people to whom interviews will be extended (via review of application information, publications, and often during telephone interviews) and again during the onsite interview process as committee and department members interact with candidates in person.
- *A personality fit.* This type of fit is often as important as academic considerations. A search committee can initially begin to gauge a candidate's demeanor based on comments provided in letters of reference. However, most committees reserve judgment

until they meet candidates during the interview process. Unfortunately, this often puts a search committee at a disadvantage and can become expensive since some candidates may seem great on paper, but are less than impressive in person. Committees often work around this limitation by holding short interviews during national or regional conferences, requesting initial telephone interviews, and by following up letters of recommendation with telephone calls to references (refer to the section Self-Presentation: Social Skills and Attire in Chapter 6).

• *Someone who is tenurable.* It is illogical and expensive to recruit and hire someone who has little chance of earning tenure. In a sense, most search committees are looking for candidates with a record or potential record of teaching and/or research that they believe will continue if that candidate is hired. The assumption is that one's past record will probably predict future performance. I've heard that some institutions hire several junior faculty yearly with the purpose of only offering tenure to one, but this type of practice appears to be the exception rather than the rule. Most institutions are searching for people who will enhance their program, earn tenure, and establish a career there.

• *A financial fit.* Because budgetary constraints must be considered, search committees have to adhere to certain salary and benefits ranges. Some institutions have more latitude than others (e.g., private institutions more than public ones), but even the most well-endowed institution must be fiscally responsible. And while salary ranges are somewhat dictated by market forces and specific institutional decisions, most committees wish to negotiate terms that are acceptable for the department/program and that will attract the best candidates for the position.

• *Service oriented.* Although the importance of service varies by institution, many, especially small liberal arts or teaching institutions, require some level of commitment on the part of new faculty. This means that committee members may wish to assess a candidate's willingness to become involved in activities such as community service, student mentoring, or institutional committee work.

• *Other issues.* A variety of other considerations may affect who is considered an ideal candidate. These may include whether the department is expanding, seeking to diversify, responding to specific departmental/program needs or reacting to a different set of university needs, or whether the committee is spearheading a search under time constraints. In some instances, decisions may be made based on factors outside your control and not germane to your specific credentials.

Given these considerations, it is your task to inform the committee that you, in fact, have the above traits and would be a perfect fit. The goal is intentionality regarding those dynamics you can influence to increase your chances of selection.

■ The Application Packet

The importance of the application packet cannot be overemphasized because the application packet is usually the first exposure search committees will have to you. The application packet should be considered a "self-presentation on paper." As such, try to make the best impression possible. Based on the initial employment advertisement, the application packet may consist of a cover letter and vita or it may consist of these documents plus a teaching portfolio, writing samples, letters of reference, transcripts, and other supporting documents. Regardless of the scope of the packet, it will serve to introduce you to prospective employers, so a great deal of effort should be made to develop a complete, professional document that is free of errors and easy to read and understand. This section focuses on how to develop each component of the typical application packet and simple strategies to make your application stand out from the rest.

The Cover Letter

The cover letter is typically the first document the search committee reads. It should easily and succinctly identify you and the position for which you are applying (this is especially important if several positions are available). Present your graduate school academic profile (name of institution, academic credentials, graduate school, areas of focus) and summarize your research or teaching interests in the first few paragraphs (depending on the type of institution to which you are applying). It is also important to

specifically mention why you think you are the best match for the
position. Letters vary in length and style, but they should reflect
your best writing. Ask faculty members in your graduate program
to review your cover letter and provide suggestions for improvements; they may discover errors that have gone unnoticed. Once a
strong cover letter has been developed, keep a standard copy on
file and revise it for each position. Be sure to change the name,
address, and content for each position. Nothing is more embarrass-
ing and potentially disqualifying than to send a cover letter meant
for one institution to another. Your letter should also include
answers to any specific questions provided in the advertisement.

Although the cover letter provides an overview of your academic experience and credentials, it should also be considered a
marketing piece because you are attempting to sell yourself as
objectively, yet compellingly, as possible. This means that balance
is key. It is important to highlight your strengths and skills relative
to the position without being self-aggrandizing. At the same time,
you will want to mention any gaps in your academic history that
are revealed by your curriculum vita. For example, if you have an
employment gap due to sickness; limited or no publications but
your dissertation is under consideration by a publisher; or you
have limited teaching, you may want to briefly note these issues.
You must decide whether such information is necessary and, if so,
how to phrase such comments so that your credibility as a candidate is not diminished.

Sample cover letters (separate examples for primarily teaching
or research institutions) with comments highlighting important
points are provided and explained below (Figures 4.5 and 4.6).
Although the focus and placement of information will vary based
on the institution to which you are applying, there are seventeen
standard items that should be included in every cover letter (see
box). Each part may be a single paragraph or several paragraphs,
depending on the amount of information you wish to present. To
help ensure conciseness and not unduly tax the reader (don't over-
whelm or bore the search committee in this initial correspondence), try to keep the cover letter under two to three pages.

Seventeen Elements of the Cover Letter

1. Name and address of contact
2. Opening request for consideration for the position
3. Type of position for which you are applying
4. List of research and teaching areas
5. Summary of dissertation research and results (if available)
6. Highlights of any critical, interesting, atypical, or groundbreaking findings
7. How dissertation work can be linked to current position
8. If ABD, expected graduation date
9. Responses to any specific questions from the advertisement
10. Summary of publications, grants, and other important academic accomplishments (remember to reverse the order of the research and teaching sections based on the type of position)
11. Summary of teaching experience
12. Summary of other academic and/or nonacademic experience and employment that can be related to the position
13. Statement about letters of recommendation (forthcoming, provided upon request)
14. Personal closing comments (it's important to personalize the letter in some way)
15. Request for an interview
16. Closing
17. List of references (provide a list of names after the closing)

Figure 4.5 Sample Cover Letter for a Teaching Institution

Candidate Profile: Recent Ph.D. applying for a psychology position at a small teaching college, performs qualitative research, and has one publication forthcoming. Candidate has taught several courses and served as a teaching assistant.

September 15, 2007

Dr. Brandon Johnson[a]
Search Committee Chair
Department of Psychology
Benjamin Franklin College
Franklin, PA 00000

Dear Dr. Brandon Johnson,

I am writing in regard to the assistant professor position in the Psychology Department[b] at Benjamin Franklin College. I am excited about potentially joining the faculty in your department. My teaching and research interests lie in the following areas: psychology and early adolescent identity, children's socialization in single-parent households, and grounded theory analysis.[c] I believe that my teaching experiences would prove especially beneficial to your department.[d] I successfully defended my dissertation research (June 3, 2007)[e,f] on the relationship between familial dynamics and subsequent proactive attitudes and behavior among early adolescents. I am particularly interested in study-ing and teaching subjects germane to early adolescent identity forma-

a. Submit letter to search committee head or contact (use a specific name, if available).
b. List title of position for which you are applying and the department.
c. List areas of teaching and research interest.
d. Request the position.
e. Briefly summarize dissertation objectives and major findings.
f. Note graduate school status (if ABD, provide expected completion date).

(Figure 4.5 continued)

tion and development beyond processes posited by classical models. Furthermore, my dissertation findings, based on life histories of ten working-class families, illustrate the importance of moving beyond deficit models when considering the experiences of children who are raised in working class, single-parent households.

I have been able to teach several courses, including Introduction to Psychology, Adolescent Psychological Behavior, and Introduction to Family Psychology. I attempt to teach in a creative, engaging manner that motivates students to think critically and apply psychological learning to everyday life. My commitment to teaching and my exemplary teaching record are reflected in consistent student evaluations that average 4.9 out of a possible 5.0 assessment (item 15 on the enclosed evaluations).[g] I consistently rank in the highest percentile in both quantitative and qualitative scoring systems used by my department. I find teaching professionally and personally exciting and rewarding. I have also had the opportunity to serve as a teaching assistant for Dr. Javi Benderson (letter of reference enclosed),[h] a master teacher and one of the leading scholars in the area of adolescent psychology. Under his tutelage, I introduced a new course to the curriculum at Smyth College that considers the psychological implications of class and race-based differences among early adolescents. This course represents the first time such a class was offered. I am eager to teach foundational courses in psychology and continue to develop courses in my research areas of interest based on the needs and objectives of your department.

As additional evidence of my commitment to teaching, I have a forthcoming article in *Teaching Psychology,* the premier teaching journal in our discipline. I am most pleased by this accomplishment because "Moving beyond Classical Paradigms to Understand Early Adolescent Experiences" represents a synthesis of my teaching and research interests. In addition, I was the recipient of the 2006 Harriet Taggert Teaching Award.[i] This campus-wide honor and $10,000 award is bestowed upon one graduate student yearly based on faculty, peer, and

g. Describe teaching experiences, evaluations, and future courses.
h. Describe unique experiences that reinforce your teaching ability.
i. List publications and grants (highlighting teaching-related items).

(Figure 4.5 continued)

student teaching evaluations. These accomplishments illustrate my ability and potential for continued contributions to teaching and mentoring in psychology. Enclosed you will find four letters of recommendation that reference my capabilities and potential. Also included are my vita, a teaching portfolio, and a writing sample.[j] It is my objective to join an academic team that is committed to exemplary teaching and mentoring, the intellectual and personal growth of students, and community engagement. I would very much appreciate an opportunity to discuss a career in the Psychology Department at Benjamin Franklin College.[k]

Sincerely,

Janice Polk

Janice Polk, Ph.D.

References
Dr. Javi Benderson
Dr. Ramona Jakes
Dr. Conyer Boyd
Dr. Lolita Clarke-Jones[l]

Enclosures

j. Mention enclosed supporting documents or those en route (mention that a teaching portfolio is enclosed).
k. Request an interview.
l. Include names of references.

Figure 4.6 Sample Cover Letter for a Research Institution

Candidate Profile: ABD applying for a sociology position, performs quantitative research, and has two publications and a grant. Candidate has taught courses and has nonacademic training that is related to the advertised position.

September 15, 2007

Dr. Jane Smith[a]
Recruitment Committee Chair
Department of Sociology
University of Baton Rouge
Baton Rouge, LA 00000

Dear Dr. Jane Smith,

Please consider the enclosed packet my formal application for the assistant professor position in the Sociology Department[b] at the University of Baton Rouge. My teaching and research interests lie in the following areas:[c] urban sociology, quantitative methods (statistics and methodology), inequality and stratification, and sociology of religion. I also possess other experience and expertise that may prove valuable in your department.[d]

My dissertation examines the degree to which structural constraints impact the agency of urban poor.[e] I am investigating whether similar circumstances, specifically a history of poverty and/or current residence in high poverty areas, generate uniform attitudinal and behavioral outcomes within and between racial/ethnic groups. Social factors and effects of gender and poverty concentration level that account for variations in attitudes and behavior are also examined. This study is being conducted using a sample of 5,790 respondents from the National Study on the Poor.

a. Submit letter to search committee head or contact (use a specific name, if available).
b. List title of position for which you are applying and the department.
c. List areas of teaching and research interest.
d. Request the position.
e. Summarize dissertation objectives and major findings.

(Figure 4.6 continued)

The existence of structural constraints that impact the life chances of urban dwellers has been well documented. Such studies associate structural dynamics with increased unemployment, community demise, sociopsychological malaise, increased female-headed households, and ultimately, poverty, in many urban communities. Another body of literature acknowledges urban plight, but focuses on the ability of residents to achieve empowerment and self-sufficiency. Urban residents are characterized as individuals who invoke agency in an attempt to overcome seemingly insurmountable odds. My research attempts to further explore the continued debate between these two explanatory camps.

Although I am currently completing my dissertation, several critical findings have already emerged.[f] Neighborhood and household poverty tend to only minimally affect the attitudes and behavior of respondents. The data also suggest that many people have attitudes and work ethics similar to those found in mainstream society. Moreover, an even stronger work ethic is evident for people engaged in a wide variety of creative, informal practices to earn money. Religion plays a central role in each of the analyses. Specifically, religious attendance tends to positively affect attitudes, behavior, and networks as does affiliations with certain denominations. However, certain religious ties tend to negatively affect attitudes, behavior, and networks. Several findings contradict existing literature. While a great deal of variability exists, the daily experiences of people who live in poor, urban neighborhoods are, in many ways, similar to those found in mainstream society. My research suggests that the overarching themes and descriptives that have been used to characterize the poor are incomplete. Given these and other results, I expect this work to provide a substantial contribution to the literature on urban living in general, and the urban poor experience in particular. These findings will also have policy-related and applied research implications. I will defend my dissertation on March 18, 2008, and graduate in June 2008.[f]

As noted in my curriculum vita, I have published two sole-author academic articles.[g] The first, "Race and Religion in the 21st Century," appeared in the spring 2005 edition of the *Journal of Religion.* The second piece, "Inequality and Public Awareness in Urban America," was

---

f. Note graduate school status (if ABD, provide expected completion date).
g. List publications and grants.

(Figure 4.6 continued)

featured in the September 2006 issue of the *Journal of Sociological Studies*. My article, "Myths About Race and the Underclass" is also currently under consideration by the *Urban Affairs Quarterly*. In addition, I was a recipient of a $25,000 dissertation research grant[g] sponsored by the Consortium to End Inequality. These research endeavors attest to my ability and potential for continued contributions to academic research, publication, policy initiatives, and successful proposal development. Plans are underway to analyze a file of qualitative and quantitative data regarding welfare reform in Atlanta, and I have written a grant proposal to study poverty and racial identity. Future research plans include continued quantitative work in the area of urban poverty.[h] Enclosed you will find three letters of recommendation that reference my capabilities and potential. Also included are my vita, copies of previous publications, and a teaching portfolio.[i]

Prior to pursuing the Ph.D. in Sociology, I was employed for over five years as a statistical analyst and consultant.[j] Much of my early career was spent providing statistical expertise to existing and potential clients, training new analysts, spearheading research and development projects, and writing technical proposals. I have also been quite involved in the community as a neighborhood activist and volunteer. I bring this level of expertise, commitment, and excitement to an academic career in research and teaching.

I attempt to teach in a creative manner that encourages critical thinking and the application of sociological theory to social phenomena.[k] My deep commitment to teaching and exemplary teaching record to date are evidenced by consistent student evaluations that average 4.8 out of a possible 5.0 assessment (item 17 on the enclosed evaluations).[k] I have instructed the following courses: Social Problems; Introduction to Sociology; Sex, Dating, and Relationships; Sexuality

g. List publications and grants.
h. Mention future publishing goals.
i. Mention enclosed supporting documents or those en route.
j. Mention previous employment and experiences related to the position.
k. Note teaching experiences, evaluations, and future courses (if not included, mention that a teaching portfolio can be provided upon request).

(Figure 4.6 continued)

and Society; Pre-Calculus; College Algebra; College Mathematics and Economics; and also served as graduate teaching assistant for an undergraduate statistics course. I consistently rank in the highest percentile in both quantitative and qualitative scoring systems used by my department. I find teaching and taking part in research projects both professionally and personally exciting and rewarding. I am eager to teach foundational courses in sociology such as Statistics and Methodology, Introduction to Sociology, Social Problems, and Race/Ethnicity. I also anticipate teaching a course that critically assesses the ways in which race, class, and gender inequality manifest globally, nationally, and locally. It would be unique in its inclusion of specific examples of inequality in the Baton Rouge area.

It is my objective to join an academic team that is committed to scholarship, research, and the intellectual and personal growth of students. I would very much appreciate an opportunity to discuss a career in the Sociology Department at the University of Baton Rouge.[l]

Sincerely,

Peter Johnson, ABD

Peter Johnson, ABD

References
Dr. Raymond Sturrie
Dr. Charles Jones
Dr. Constance Carlilse[m]

Enclosures

l.   Request an interview.
m. Include names of references.

Curriculum Vita

Although the cover letter introduces you to the search committee, the vita is possibly the most important document in an application packet because it provides a detailed, yet concise, profile of your academic experience. Search committees, especially those that receive a large number of applications for one or several positions, often initially only request a cover letter and academic vita. These documents can provide a quick assessment of a candidate's academic fit and writing ability, and is often used to reduce the pool of candidates to an acceptable number who are then asked to provide additional documentation for further consideration. You have the opportunity to construct a vita that accentuates those aspects of your academic career that are the most positive. The curriculum vita represents a historical account of your academic and professional career. The vita is "self-presentation" on paper. It is often the first detailed glimpse a search committee will have of you. A vita can be a door opener because it can be used to distinguish between individuals in a group of worthy candidates. The vita is a critical source of personal and professional praise—it is no place for false modesty. A vita differs from a resume in several important ways. First, a resume represents a career summary and should be no longer than several pages. However, a vita has no specific length restrictions—the goal is to accurately represent your experiences in academia. A three-page vita is just as acceptable as a seven-page vita. Second, although a vita should focus on your academic experiences, relevant nonacademic information should also be included, especially if it strengthens your profile as a well-rounded candidate.

Because such weight is placed on the vita to make initial candidate selections, it is important that you spend sufficient time developing a vita that accurately reflects your experiences, skills, and ability. Information from the vita should correspond to comments made in the cover letter, teaching portfolio, and other supporting documents, and emphasize strengths (e.g., publications) over growth areas (e.g., limited teaching experience). Thoroughly check the vita for typographical errors and format inconsistencies (review an actual hardcopy by hand). Also ask several detail-oriented people to review it. As one additional strategy, it may be helpful to have someone who is *not* associated with academia to review your vita to provide another perspective and comment on its overall level of readability and format. You may also have several versions of the same vita that are arranged differently to highlight certain areas based on specific job postings. In such cases, it is important to code the different vitas so that they can easily be distinguished. In general, the vita should be dated so that, as additional information is added, you are sure the most current version is in use. Although the format may vary, a curriculum vita should include the following sections:

- Demographics: include an e-mail address and cellular phone number
- Education (undergraduate as well as graduate school)
- Dissertation information and committee chairperson (dissertation title and expected graduation date if you are ABD)
- Areas of interest
- Publications (academic and relevant nonacademic)
- Honors and grants
- Courses taught or that you would like to teach (link to the teaching portfolio)
- Other related positions you have held (academic and nonacademic, paid and unpaid)
- Names of references (include telephone numbers and e-mail addresses)

Format your vita so that it is easy to read and visually appealing. The structure of a vita will vary from person to person and there is no one correct way to develop a vita (refer to Figures 4.7 and 4.8 for examples based on teaching- or research-focused formats). However, here are a few practical suggestions that may help you design a more reader-friendly vita that also highlights your best assets:

- *List your publications on the first page.* Because establishing a publishing record is usually essential if you wish to be most viable on the job market, if you have done so, it is best to highlight that accomplishment. Presenting your publications on the first page means that they will stand out in the document and also be easy for readers to locate. This strategy enables a search committee to quickly see that, as a graduate student, you have already begun to contribute to the literature in your discipline.

• *Separate academic from nonacademic publications.* Although you may list all of your publications in the same section, it is best to use subheadings to distinguish between academic articles, nonacademic articles, and book reviews. This will prevent the search committee and other readers from having to search through a list of publications to identify academic articles (which can be tedious). This step may seem small, but it will help make your vita more reader friendly.

• *Separate publications from presentations.* Some candidates decide to place all academic-related material under the same heading within their vitas. Thus articles, both academic and nonacademic, as well as conference presentations, are lumped together under one heading. Given that some search committees want to identify your academic writing quickly, it can become very tedious to have to search for them in a maze of other works. In addition, separating your presentations will reinforce material from the teaching portfolio and illustrate your strength as a teacher/speaker.

• *Provide lists in chronological order.* Publications, conference presentations, courses taught, awards, and grants should be listed with the most recent first and move backward in time. This format increases the likelihood that a search committee will be drawn immediately to the most recent work and lists can more easily be updated continually via word processing.

• *Include works in progress.* List forthcoming publications with an approximate publication date in a separate subsection under "Academic Publications." You may also elect to include works that are near completion and soon to be submitted; however, be careful not to appear to be using this information as filler.

• *Avoid filler.* As mentioned in the suggestion above, you want to avoid appearing to add information on your vita that does not reflect existing academic accomplishments and specific achievements. Most search committees are not expecting ten-page vitas from new candidates. Be confident in your achievements to date and concisely provide them on the vita.

• *Include honors and grants immediately following publications.* Again, this strategy will draw the reader's eye quickly to your most impressive academic achievements. Even if the grants resulted in small amounts of funding, they should still be included because they remind the reader that you have been able to locate outside funding and thus plan to do so if hired. Be sure to also include grant titles and funding sources.

• *Include related and nontraditional employment.* If you are applying for a position as an assistant professor in a political science department and you spent two summers serving as a political science tutor for disadvantaged high school students, consider including this experience on your vita. Not only does it illustrate your ability to teach political science, but it shows your willingness to take part in community service—two central elements in the careers of many academics. Or, if you worked your way through a master's program as a rodeo clown, this makes for interesting reading. And although it is not directly related to the academic position, it, in combination with your academic credentials, will definitely cause you to stand out among other candidates. If you possess atypical or extensive research skills, include them here as well.

• *Include postdoctoral experiences in the "education" section of the vita.*

• *Include service-related experiences.* If you have been involved in leadership roles within your department, took part in conference committees or subcommittees, or helped organize a regional conference, include summary statements about these service activities. They support your well-roundedness as a candidate.

Figure 4.7 Curriculum Vita for a Teaching Position

THOMAS A. TILLIS
Curriculum Vita

Office Address
Johnson K. Smyth College
Department of Family Studies
Social Sciences Building
Smyth, NY 00000
999-999-9999
ttillis@smyth.edu

Home Address
212-B Center Ave.
Smyth, NY 00000
999-999-9999

Research and Teaching Interests
Family Studies; Race, Class, and Gender; Qualitative Methodology

Education
Johnson K. Smyth College, Smyth, NY
    Ph.D., Family Studies, Fall 2007

Morehouse College, Atlanta, Georgia
    B.A., Psychology, June 2000

Current Positions
• Graduate Teaching, Johnson K. Smyth College, Smyth, NY,
    September 2003 to present
    Responsibilities: instructing, keeping attendance records, grading all
    course papers, holding office hours, assisting the professor in creat-
    ing and maintaining a class environment conducive to learning.

• Peer-group Crisis Leader, YMCA, Smyth, NY,
    January 2005–December 2005
    Responsibilities: successfully mentoring at-risk male students ages
    12–18 years old from poor families, coordinating weekly educational
    and recreational activities, mediating crises among students, moni-
    toring academic progress of student members, and serving as the liai-
    son to the YMCA Director.

(continues)

(Figure 4.7 continued)

Teaching Experiences

• Courses Taught

Introduction to Family Studies, Johnson K. Smyth College,
Spring 2004, Spring 2005

Family Inequality in the United States, Johnson K. Smyth College,
Fall 2004, Fall 2005

Research Methods in the Social Sciences, Johnson K. Smyth College,
Spring 2006

• Other Teaching Experience

Introduction to Family Studies, Johnson K. Smyth College, Fall 2003
(served as teaching assistant, Instructor Dr. Paul Primer)

Graduate Research Methods in the Social Sciences, Johnson K. Smyth
College, Spring 2007 (served as teaching assistant, Instructor Dr.
Levi Swanson)

Courses Prepared to Teach

Introduction to Family Studies; Family Inequality in the United States;
Research Methods in the Social Sciences; Race, Class, and Gender
Issues in Contemporary Families; Qualitative Methods for Studying
Diverse Families

Academic Publications

"A Case Study Analysis of Middle Class Families in Brooklyn, NY:
Teaching the Familiar," forthcoming, *National Journal of Teaching*.

Work in Progress

"Class Distinctions and Family Dynamics in Rural New York"

Grants and Honors

2007   Department of Family Studies Distinguished Teaching Award
2004   Johnson K. Smyth College Graduate Teaching Award, $2,500
2000   Phi Beta Kappa, Delta of Georgia Chapter

Paper Presentations

"Qualitative Perspectives on Hispanic Family Life," presented at the
Family and Cultural Studies Conference in San Francisco,
California, August, 2006.

(Figure 4.7 continued)

"Negotiating Poverty: An Analysis of Familial Challenges Among
Rural New Yorkers," presented at the National Cultural Studies
Symposium in San Diego, California, June, 2004.

"What's New About the Family: Nontraditional Paradigms and
Approaches," presented at the Family and Cultural Studies
Conference in Richmond, Virginia, August, 2003.

Previous Academic Positions
Adjunct Professor: Social Work, City College, Alfred, NY,
January 2003–December 2004

Professional Memberships
National Teachers Association
Conference of Cultural and Family Studies

References

Dr. Paul Primer
Dept. of Family Studies
Johnson K. Smyth College
Social Sciences Building
Smyth, NY 00000
999-999-9999
pprimer@smyth.edu

Dr. Levi Swanson
Dept. of Family Studies
Johnson K. Smyth College
Social Sciences Building
Smyth, NY 00000
999-999-9999
lswanson@smyth.edu

Dr. Saundra Kaulder
Dept. of Family Studies
Johnson K. Smyth College
Social Sciences Building
Smyth, NY 00000
999-999-9999
skaulder@smyth.edu

Figure 4.8 Curriculum Vita for a Research Position

SAMANTHA BANKS
Curriculum Vita

Office Address
Georgia Institute of Technology
Department of Systems Engineering
Stephenson Plaza
Atlanta, Georgia 00000
999-999-9999
sbanks@gtech.edu

Home Address
413 Main Street
Atlanta, Georgia 00000
999-999-9999

Research and Teaching Interests
Linear Programming; Fuzzy Set Analysis; Statistics and Methodology

Education
Georgia Institute of Technology, Atlanta, Georgia
   Ph.D., Operations Research, Fall 2006

Emory University, Atlanta, Georgia
   M.S., Mathematics, March 1995

Boston College, Boston, Massachusetts
   B.A., Mathematics, June 1993

Current Positions
Graduate teaching assistant, Georgia Institute of Technology, Atlanta, Georgia, February 2004

Focus Group Coordinator, Urban Poverty Center, Atlanta, Georgia, January 2004

Academic Publications
"Fuzzy Set Analysis in Real Time," *Quantitative Studies* 21(4): 240–255, 2004.

Papers Under Review
"Teaching Linear Programming to Undergraduates as an Elective," *Teaching in the Sciences.*

(continues)

Work in Progress
"Migration Patterns and Economic Differentials in the South," to be
submitted in March 2008.
"Long Distance Learning and Linear Programming," to be submitted in
December 2007.

Grants and Honors
2006   Georgia Institute of Technology Research Grant, "Fuzzy Set
Analysis of Rural Immigration Rates," $10,000

2005   National Science Foundation Grant, "A Longitudinal Study of
Out-Migration Patterns in Georgia, 1900–1990," $35,000

Paper Presentations
"Quantitative Perspectives on Urban Life," presented at the National
Science Meeting in San Francisco, California, August, 2005.
"Where Are Women Working? An Analysis of Urban and Rural
Differences in Occupational and Industry Distributions," presented at
the American Mathematical Association Meeting in Atlanta, Georgia,
April, 2005.
"Fuzzy Set Analysis as a Paradigm for the 21st Century," presented at
the National Science Meeting in New Orleans, Louisiana, April,
2004.
"The Implications of Fuzzy Set Analysis for Integrating Systems," pre-
sented at the Southern Mathematical Society Meeting in Baton
Rouge, Louisiana, March, 2004.

Honors
2005   American Mathematical Association Honors Award Recipient
2005   Southern Mathematical Society Competition: 2nd Place
2005   Pi Gamma Xi International Honor Society
2005   Blue Key National Honor Fraternity
2005   Alpha Kappa Kappa Research Grant, Georgia Institute of
Technology
2004   Georgia Institute of Technology Outstanding Teaching Award

Courses Taught
Introduction to Calculus, Georgia Institute of Technology, Winter 2005

(continues)

(Figure 4.8 continued)

Introduction to Fuzzy Sets, Georgia Institute of Technology, Spring 2005

College Algebra, Dekalb Institute of Technology, 2002–2004

Real Numbers, Georgia Institute of Technology, Fall 2004

Linear Programming I and II, Georgia Institute of Technology, Fall 2004

Previous Academic Positions
Adjunct Professor: Math/Economics, Dekalb Technical Institute, Dekalb, Georgia, April 2002–December 2004

Professional Memberships
American Mathematical Association
Southern Mathematical Society

Dissertation Committee/References

Dr. Denny Washington
Mathematics Department
Georgia Institute of Technology
Stephenson Plaza
Atlanta, Georgia 00000
999-999-9999
Socdw@gtech.edu

Dr. Tom Cantel
Department of Industrial & Systems Engineering
Georgia Institute of Technology
Stephenson Plaza
Atlanta, Georgia 00000
999-999-9999
tcantel@gtech.edu

Dr. Jean Phillipe
Department of Industrial & Systems Engineering
Georgia Institute of Technology
Stephenson Plaza
Atlanta, Georgia 00000
999-999-9999
jp@gtech.edu

Teaching Portfolio

It is quite common for institutions to require candidates to submit a teaching portfolio as a standard component of the application packet. Even if it is not initially requested, candidates that move through the early phases of the selection process should expect a portfolio to eventually be requested. Because developing a comprehensive teaching portfolio requires a great deal of effort, you should begin compiling it early in your graduate career and augment it with information as you progress through the program. It may be beneficial for a cohort to start a teaching portfolio support group in which they collaborate and assist each other in developing portfolios. Detailed information on developing a teaching portfolio is provided in Chapter 5.

Letters of Recommendation

Like the vita, strong letters of reference from well-respected academicians will help distinguish you from other candidates. In order to locate people to write such letters, you must establish meaningful, positive relationships with faculty members in your department and discipline who will vouch for your academic progress, potential, and character. Most institutions require three to four letters of reference. It is generally expected that your dissertation chairperson and other committee members will provide them. Letters from the graduate program director, department head or chair, or noted scholars in the discipline are also impressive. Who should you ask to write letters on your behalf? One strategy would be to ask the four members of your dissertation committee to write the majority of the letters, then request letters from people such as the department head or that well-known scholar in your subfield only for those schools where references from them might provide an additional boost to your application packet. It can also be impressive to include a letter from an external academic mentor to illustrate your level of professional engagement at the international, national, or regional level. Be sure to record who is writing letters and for which institutions on your application schedule (example provided later in this chapter) so that you can easily and quickly keep track. Note that the contact information for those people who will write the majority of your letters of reference should be included on your vita.

It is most important that you request letters from people who are familiar with your academic performance and who know you well (always provide letter writers with a current copy of your vita so that it can be referred to in their letters). Remember, ask people who will recommend you highly—other candidates are doing the same and this is expected. Letters that are less than glowing or unusually brief are suspicious because the search committee is aware that *you made the choice* to select this person as a reference. In some cases, a brief letter is excused if it is from, for example, the top scholar in your discipline who is known to be extremely busy and "unattainable." In this instance, simply being able to garner a letter from such an individual may be impressive.

Send your requests at the same time and give your references sufficient time (at least two to three weeks per letter) to write letters. To facilitate the process, give them the list of institution names and corresponding job advertisements. Clearly identify your requested deadline and how the reference should be provided (e.g., via separate mail, given to you and mailed with the entire application packet). It may also be wise to set the deadline *two weeks prior* to the actual application submission deadline so that, if they forget or get busy and write the letter "late," it will still meet the deadline. This latter strategy is important because faculty are often very busy and may be asked to write several letters for you as well as for other graduate students. Also request that letter writers send you a confirmation e-mail when the letter has been completed and/or mailed. If you have not received the confirmation e-mail the day before your established deadline, send a short reminder e-mail asking whether additional information is needed to complete the letter. If the person had forgotten to write the letter, this will be a subtle reminder (and remember, the letter will not be late because of the way you set the deadline). Don't be afraid to ask whether a person has completed the letter—just do so once in a nonconfrontational manner. Remember, letter writing is one of the responsibilities of faculty and people involved in your academic career expect to do it. Because it is common to use the same faculty members repeatedly, they may develop a standard reference letter format for you and revise it based on the advertisement requirements. Providing them with the appropriate information in a timely manner will help facilitate the process and ensure that they are more willing to assist.

When mailing letters, be sure to specifically follow the instructions in the advertisement. Some schools may not mind if sealed, official letters are included in the application packet, while others specifically request that letters be mailed separately. In other instances, committees only request the names of potential references. Also, only send the number of letters requested in the advertisement. However, if the institution does not request a specific number of letters, candidates who are fortunate enough to have four to five people who will provide good recommendations may elect to have all these people send letters.

On a practical note, if an institution does not request that letters be sent under separate mailing, ask references to provide their letters in sealed envelopes with their signatures across the seal and to give the letters directly to you. Letters can then be placed in the application packet with the other supporting documents and mailed at one time. This strategy ensures that the search committee receives a complete application packet and minimizes lost or late letters. This is important because, in most cases, a committee cannot fully evaluate you without letters of recommendation. If your letters are late (or are lost in the mail), your application packet may be set aside.

Writing Samples and Other Supporting Documents

In addition to the cover letter and vita, you should expect to provide a writing sample in the completed application packet—especially if you are applying for a research position. A writing sample will provide evidence of your scholarship and ability to write in an academic fashion. If publishing is a major expectation, candidates who have already done so are usually considered impressive. Some institutions will only require one writing sample; others may want several. If you do not have a publication, it may still be prudent to provide a sample of your best work from a certain seminar or research project (be sure to have a faculty member review it first). Although it will not be considered on par with an actual publication, it will serve to expose readers to your writing potential. If you have one publication, whether it is single- or co-authored, include a neat, clean copy in the packet. If you are fortunate enough to have multiple publications, seek advice from your graduate adviser regarding which manuscript(s) to use. However, be sure that any sample you provide represents your best work.

Some institutions may also require you to provide additional supporting documents, such as official transcripts from all academic institutions you have attended. To fulfill such requests it is important to give other institutions sufficient time to process the requests and mail them to the interested schools. Save time by requesting at least five copies of supporting documents from each institution at the beginning of your search. Also consider the timing factor to make sure all supporting documents reach the prospective institution before the deadline.

■ Other Application Strategies

Once you have decided on the position(s) to which you are going to apply, the goal is to distinguish yourself from other candidates. Provide information about skills and accomplishments that might be impressive to a search committee and increase your desirability. The following types of accomplishments can be highlighted:

- A stellar grade point average
- Special courses taught
- Internships, grants, fellowships, study abroad experiences
- Service learning
- Mentoring and tutoring
- Volunteer work
- Earlier careers that enhance your current skill set
- Roles that emphasize management and leadership skills
- Coordinating conference meetings and sessions
- Other academic honors (Phi Beta Kappa and other honor societies)

Many of the above accomplishments can easily be included on your vita. Also mention particularly impressive items in the cover letter. By highlighting and emphasizing special skills, strengths, and experiences, you can set yourself apart from other candidates and improve your chances of getting an interview. Finally, once the application packet has been developed, ask several faculty members to review it in its entirety (cover letter, vita, teaching portfolio, and supporting documents) to assess its overall presentation, content, structure, and flow. Be open to suggestions for improvements and be prepared to justify each part of the application packet.

■ Sample Application Schedule

Because you will probably apply to a wide variety of institutions, an organized format is needed to keep track of where you have applied and what documents have been provided. This information should be consistently and accurately maintained. An example of one possible tracking method is provided below (Figure 4.9). A similar schedule can be created using a spreadsheet program such as Excel. The schedule should include the name of each institution and a brief summary of the position. Checks or comments should be placed in the cells to correspond to the application documents that were provided. Finally, the application deadline should be noted. A special column to identify whether letters of reference are to be mailed separately will also help you remember to remind faculty members about their reference letters. A column should always be included to note the final status of the application (interview, rejected, short list, offer made). Additional columns can be added for special considerations. The important point is to document each item provided to each institution. This information is also helpful if a search committee representative notifies you that certain documents have not been received because you have a record of what has been provided and when.

Figure 4.9 Sample Application Schedule

Institution Name	Position	Cover Letter	Vita	Teaching Portfolio	Letters of Recommendation	Other	Special Notes	Deadline	Status
Smith College	Inequality and gender	Sent	Sent	Later	4 (mailed separately)	Transcript	None	2-4-07	

5

The Teaching Portfolio

In most institutions, professors are expected to teach as well as perform research. Historically, certain institutions placed greater emphasis on research than teaching; at others, the opposite was true. Although this pattern still exists at some colleges and universities, the trend is now toward hiring candidates who are adept at both teaching and research. If you are preparing to enter the job market, it would be wise to be able to document both research accomplishments and teaching skills. A teaching portfolio is the best way to do the latter. There are several exceptional texts that cover this topic in general. See P. Seldin, *Successful Use of Teaching Portfolios* (1993) and *The Teaching Portfolio: A Practical Guide to Improved Performance and Promotion/Tenure Decisions* (2004); and J. Davis and L. Swift, "Teaching Portfolios at a Research University" (1995). This chapter focuses on how to develop a teaching portfolio to specifically enhance the marketability of new job candidates.

The concept of the teaching portfolio was developed by the Canadian Association of University Teachers (CAUT) in the early 1970s. The term "portfolio" was borrowed from photographers, but eventually portfolio became "dossier" (that term was not used in the United States due to its sinister connotations) (see Christopher Knapper, "The Origins of Teaching Portfolios" [1995]). CAUT developed a guidebook for creating the dossier/portfolio, which gradually spread to the United Kingdom and the United States. Currently, around five hundred colleges and universities in the United States and Canada are using portfolios.

This chapter presents the components of a teaching portfolio and examples of its various parts. You are reminded of one important fact at the outset—developing a teaching portfolio can be time consuming with little immediate direct feedback or reward; therefore, it is best accomplished within a group setting. A number of portfolio "experts" recommend bringing in a consultant who can work with graduate students and faculty. This may be the preferred plan, but not always feasible. A department and/or institution may not have the money or inclination to bring in an outside consultant. Graduate students and interested faculty can get started without the aid of an experienced guide. For example, within the Sociology Department at Georgia State University a group of faculty and graduate students started a "teaching portfolio support group" that met every third week. At each meeting, people exchanged material that they had written, and critiqued each other's work. Revised documents were brought back to the group for further review and revisions. Members progressed at different rates, but the feedback and support from others were essential components of the process; efforts resulted in teaching portfolios that were central to each student locating a position.

■ The Importance of a Teaching Portfolio for Candidates

Simply put, a teaching portfolio is a series of documents, typically provided in booklet form that recreates your teaching strengths, accomplishments, and goals. It is to teaching what a curriculum vita is to research. Creating and maintaining a teaching portfolio takes time and energy, two factors that are usually in short supply for most graduate students. However, in today's employment arena, a teaching portfolio is quite important. Why? The teaching portfolio complements your other academic credentials in presenting you as a well-rounded candidate. Remember, in most instances, you are competing for positions that require you to do research and teach. While your vita and copies of publications provide support for the former, they do not necessarily support the latter (unfortunately, there are academics who produce excellent scholarship, but who are less than effective in the classroom). The teaching portfolio can substantiate the latter skill. A teaching portfolio benefits candidates entering the job market in several ways.

• *Getting a job.* Most candidates are expected to have some teaching experience. Even research-oriented institutions usually require basic aptitude in the classroom; some colleges require extensive research *as well as* exceptional teaching skills. Most search committees are interested in whether you have taught and how well you performed in the classroom. A well-constructed teaching portfolio will give all interested parties insight into your teaching philosophy, style, and accomplishments. And by constructing your own portfolio, you are able to present teaching approaches, accomplishments, and goals in the best light. In addition, review of teaching portfolios provides search committees with another formal method to distinguish the best prepared candidates from a potentially large pool of applicants.

• *Documenting teaching effectiveness.* The portfolio should include specific criteria by which your teaching effectiveness can be assessed as well as several modes of evaluation. Possibilities include: faculty, student, peer, and numeric evaluations.

• *Enhancing teaching in anticipation of a new position.* Experienced teachers often run the risk of becoming stagnant and predictable in their teaching. This can also happen to graduate students who are forced to juggle teaching, research, and accountability to a variety of faculty members. After teaching the introductory American History course for the tenth time, it becomes easy to forget your teaching goals. Constructing a teaching portfolio allows the experienced teacher to reexamine personal teaching philosophy, style, and goals. In contrast, constructing a portfolio motivates graduate students to develop these statements, skills, and tools. The exercise will aid in determining those subjects you teach well, growth areas, and courses you are interested in teaching. Developing a teaching portfolio will help you develop a comprehensive portrait of your pedagogy as a teacher. It is important to have a good understanding of your role as teacher before you enter the classroom in an official capacity in a new position. You may find the exercise both intimidating and exhilarating, but working on a portfolio will help you become a better, more thoughtful teacher.

• *Helping departments/programs identify "fit."* Review of your teaching portfolio by a search committee will quickly inform them of your teaching credentials, strengths, topics of focus, and specific courses previously taught, as well as other courses you are qualified to teach. This information can be compared directly to the departmental/program needs to determine whether you are a good fit for the position.

• *Showing time-management skills.* Candidates who have been able to effectively balance teaching, research, and other graduate school requirements will be most impressive. A teaching portfolio can be used to show your ability to perform well in the classroom. This, in combination with other application information, illustrates to search committees that you have already begun to effectively perform those central duties of a professor.

Although teaching portfolios can also be used when seeking promotion and tenure or to renew and revitalize one's teaching, these are issues that will come later in your career. The present objective is to develop a portfolio to increase your competitive edge in the market.

■ Principles of the Teaching Portfolio

There is no one way to construct a portfolio. You will want to modify the models presented in this chapter to suit your own experiences. The goal is to develop a teaching portfolio that accurately and completely reflects *your* teaching experiences, goals, strategies, and objectives. However, in constructing a portfolio there are a few general principles to consider:

• *The audience.* Is the primary audience a recruitment or search committee at a college or university to which you are applying or for fellow faculty members? For example, most candidates have some strong student evaluations and some that are not quite so strong. People who are trying to improve their teaching may choose to include the mixed evaluations because they want to remind themselves about a particularly challenging class. But people who are entering the academic job market may not feel it necessary to include comments from disgruntled students.

• *Presentation.* Develop a consistent plan for organizing materials and then adhere to it. From the Table of Contents the reader should be able to locate material easily. The portfolio should encompass your time in graduate school (i.e., four or five years). If the period differs (e.g., you were an adjunct before entering graduate school), specify the length of time the portfolio covers.

• *Let your personality and writing style be heard.* In some cases the portfolio will be the first introduction a search committee has to you as a teacher or instructor. The portfolio will speak for you; so write in a style that reflects who you are. There is no law that says that portfolios have to be drenched in academic jargon.

Figure 5.1 in the following section of this volume presents a representative Table of Contents. Remember that what is included is, at least in part, a function of the purpose for constructing a portfolio (i.e., applying for a position, seeking tenure, improving teaching skills). After presenting the Table of Contents, each section is discussed and illustrations are provided.

■ Components of a Teaching Portfolio

A teaching portfolio should be considered one complete document. Each section should be logically linked to and reinforce other sections. The parts of the portfolio should also flow so that the reader gets a specific, comprehensive picture of the kind of teacher you are (or are trying to become). Information in one section that seems to contradict information in another section should be clearly explained so that the reader does not question the portfolio's validity.

Statement of Teaching Philosophy, Goals, and Strategies

The major function of this section is to introduce your general educational philosophy. This section is the most difficult to

---

**Figure 5.1 Sample Table of Contents
for a Teaching Portfolio**

Mary Malone
Smith University
Department of Sociology

Table of Contents

1. Statement of Teaching Philosophy, Goals, and Strategies
2. Teaching Responsibilities
3. Representative Teaching Materials: Syllabi, Handouts, Study Guides, Examinations
4. Evaluations of Teaching
5. Evidence of Student Accomplishments
6. Teaching-Related Activities
7. Future Teaching Goals and Plans
8. Curriculum Vita
9. Appendices
   Appendix A: Course Syllabi
   Appendix B: Tests and Assignments
   Appendix C: Nonprinted Materials
   Appendix D: Student Evaluations

---

write; however, once written, it should be used to inform all the other materials in the portfolio. If you have not reflected on your philosophy, goals, and strategies, you might start by examining past and current syllabi, assignments, and exams. Anyone who has ever taught has a teaching philosophy, though you may not have articulated or documented it. In order to develop this statement, evaluate your teaching materials. What were you attempting to accomplish? What teaching techniques were used to accomplish these goals? There are three parts to a teaching statement: the general teaching philosophy, teaching goals, and teaching strategies. This statement should include the general philosophy of education, skills, and attitudes that you wish to relay, specific strategies used to accomplish these

Fourteen Things to Remember
When Developing a Teaching Statement

- **General Characteristics**
  1. The ideological basis for the rest of the portfolio
  2. Short (two paragraphs maximum)
  3. Engaging
  4. Represents who you are as an instructor

- **Philosophy**
  5. Most general part of statement
  6. Broad pedagogical philosophy
  7. Avoid glittering generalities
  8. Punch up statement with distinctive words and phrases

- **Teaching Goals**
  9. Must reflect teaching philosophy
  10. Should be reasonably specific

- **Teaching Strategies**
  11. Should reflect philosophy and goals
  12. Be specific

- **Teaching Responsibilities**
  13. Introduce this section with a brief description of the department and your general responsibilities within it (e.g., undergraduate coordinator, honors instructor)
  14. Provide a brief description of each course you regularly teach. Describe the basic approach to the course and some of the teaching strategies used. Provide an explanation if the approach to a course is dramatically different from your philosophy/goals statement.

goals, and assessment strategies employed to evaluate the success of your teaching. It should not be more than one page in length, though some people condense the material into a few paragraphs.

Statement of teaching philosophy. This statement need not be longer than a paragraph, but it should succinctly express your basic pedagogical approach. You may not have given much consideration to your teaching philosophy. Those who have not should ask themselves a few questions including, What is the purpose of teaching? Is it to instruct, motivate, reward, enhance? Why is teaching in general and teaching in my field in particular worthwhile? What do I hope and anticipate that students will take from my classes? Once you have determined your teaching philosophy, compose the statement. Try to stay away from glittering generalities, but punch up the statement with words or phrases that are distinctive. Remember, this statement is probably the first part of the teaching portfolio that others will read. Edit the statement for superfluous or redundant words.

Statement of teaching goals. Teaching goals should be briefly presented in this section. These goals may be reasonably specific and should reflect your teaching philosophy. For example, if you write in your philosophy statement that you support a commitment to social action on the part of students who take your class, then it will be important to include student development of social action projects as one of the teaching goals.

Statement of teaching strategies. The general teaching strategies you employ should reflect your philosophy and goals. Oral reports, field trips, weekly quizzes, or term papers are just a few of the strategies that can be utilized. These strategies should be reflected in syllabi, exams, and handouts.

* * *

The sections on philosophy, goals, and strategies represent your overall approach to teaching. Taken together, they should present a unified picture of your teaching values and aspirations. The final section summarizes teaching responsibilities and the courses that you have regularly taught. Be sure to carefully review the statement for punctuation errors and formatting problems. See Figures 5.2 and 5.3 for two examples of teaching philosophy statements.

Figure 5.2 Sample Teaching Statement, Abbreviated

This is a sample of an abbreviated version of a teaching philosophy statement. Your statement can be fairly general or fairly specific, but it should include more than generalities. Writing a teaching philosophy statement will help you determine what you think you are teaching.

General Philosophy of Teaching. I believe that learning and teaching are interactive experiences best accomplished in an open classroom where students are free to challenge both the texts and me. I see myself as facilitating the intellectual growth of students by providing learning resources and feedback on products of their academic efforts.

Teaching Goals. There are four kinds of learning: declarative, procedural, conditional, and reflective. In all of my courses I teach my students a number of skills they can use in other courses as well as outside the classroom. For example, in the Introductory Statistics course, my students learn how to compute the three measures of central tendency.

Teaching Strategies. In order to teach my students how to compute and use the three measures of central tendency, I provide them with a simple data set. Working in groups, they decide which variables they plan to use. After selecting two or three variables, they compute the mean, median, and mode for those variables. After they have completed this exercise successfully, we discuss how their results can be interpreted.

Providing Feedback. One major question on the final examination involves asking students to compute the mean, median, and mode for variables from another data set and interpret their findings.

Figure 5.3 Sample Teaching Statement, Detailed

This sample statement reflects the teaching philosophy of a junior faculty member. The writer references specific courses and teaching approaches and uses animated words to invoke excitement.

I. General Philosophy of Teaching

The essence of teaching involves encouraging critical thinking, evoking an emotional response, stimulating self-reflection, inviting laughter, welcoming challenge, and invoking informed activity in the world. To teach effectively is to continually and consistently challenge students. I invite students to imagine realities outside their own. I encourage them to move beyond their current, often comfortable, frame of reference and begin to examine the world as an anthropologist. Passion and preparation must be present if this type of teaching is to take place. I try to help students gain a body of knowledge and better understand the world, others, and themselves. The ultimate goal is to take advantage of each teachable moment so that students are able to effectively combine their passion and knowledge in the "real world." I want students to become excited about anthropology and how it can be used to enhance their lives and the lives of others.

II. My Teaching Goals

A primary goal is to shape the teaching/learning experience for students based on the context, course topic, and overall course level. While course standards are high, students feel free to query each other and me in a positive environment that stimulates analysis of seemingly everyday social phenomena. Students are encouraged to rely on a variety of skills, yet I especially encourage the use of group discussions. Students learn because it is assumed that they can learn, they participate because the milieu encourages it, and they critique because they are given the proper tools to do so. For me, teaching reflects a dual purpose that can enhance my life and the lives of my students.

III. Teaching Strategies

A central focus in my classes (e.g., The World and Its People, Introduction to Anthropology) is for students to fully understand and be able to explain certain theories and anthropological perspectives (i.e., the debate surrounding nature vs. nurture). I also want them to be able to apply these theories and perspectives to real world situations and to attempt to develop their own theories. Lectures, group projects, outside speakers, and nontraditional methods such as the use of multicultural music are used as strategies.

Statement of Teaching Responsibilities

This section of your portfolio should include descriptions of the courses you have regularly taught in the context of the department's needs and requirements. The amount of information that may be presented here varies greatly, based on the intended use of the portfolio. For candidates applying for positions, this section should include a detailed description of courses taught, roles, and responsibilities. First, some information about the department is needed. For example, size of faculty, teaching expectations, department specialties, whether you were expected to teach across the curriculum, whether courses are cross-listed, whether it is an advanced degree-granting program, or whether there is a specific departmental focus. The answers to these and related questions will give the reader some background for understanding your role in the teaching responsibilities of the department.

The example in Figure 5.4 below describes the teaching responsibilities of a faculty member in sociology. The author indicates whether or not the courses are graduate or undergraduate and required or service courses (graduate students developing a teaching portfolio would not be expected to have taught a graduate course). The author also identifies those courses that she developed. For each course or group of related courses, briefly describe the content of the course and, perhaps, some of the teaching strategies utilized. Again, make sure that the course descriptions are compatible with the general teaching philosophy and goals. If the course content is not compatible, explain why. For example, you might emphasize that while you only give essay exams, the department mandates a multiple choice standardized final examination in an introductory course.

When describing the courses that are taught, avoid reproducing the catalog descriptions, which are often dull, vague, and formulaic. Try to give the reader a feel for what you try to "do" in the course. It is useful to indicate both the depth and breadth of the material that is covered, as well as particular emphases that are made. Try to keep the discipline jargon to a minimum and be specific about what is covered. If a strategy or approach works particularly well, be sure to mention it. The teaching portfolio is no place for false modesty. Some departments offer both graduate

Figure 5.4 Sample Statement of Teaching Responsibilities

My department offers undergraduate, masters, and Ph.D. programs in sociology. At all three levels we require a core of theory, methods, and statistics courses. At the graduate level, we offer two specialties: Social Conflict and Inequality, and Family and the Life Course. My teaching responsibilities include both undergraduate and graduate courses.

Undergraduate Responsibilities. I teach four courses: Introduction to Sociology, Sex Roles in Modern Society, Gays and Lesbians in Society, and Popular Culture.

Introduction to Sociology. I consider this the most important course in the department because it is students' (and potential majors') first exposure to sociology. My primary goal is to show students the sociological in contrast to the psychological perspective. At the beginning of the course I provide each student with a packet of raw data about lottery players in Georgia. During the quarter they work in groups to develop and test hypotheses about the relationship between player characteristics and problem gambling. By the end of the quarter I hope they understand what a sociological problem is and how a sociologist might gather and analyze data to study the problem.

Sex Roles in Modern Society and Gays and Lesbians in Society. I developed both courses, the first at the request of the department chairperson and the second at the request of a gay student who thought there should be at least one course on campus about lesbians and gays. The content of the sex roles course has changed over the years. I begin with an introduction to the biology of gender differentiation and theories of gender stratification. One core area is the role of men and women cross-culturally and another is the relationship between religion and conceptions of male and female identity. I use group projects, films, and a slide presentation on cross-cultural gender roles that I created.

The gay and lesbian course is still evolving, and I am not yet satisfied with its content or my style of presentation. I concentrate on the following core areas: the essentialism vs. social construction debate, the measure of sexual orientation, and the history of lesbian-gay social movements. I use films and group presentations and also give the students the option of doing service learning for course credit.

(continues)

(Figure 5.4 continued)

Popular Culture. Popular Culture is an area that is neglected by most sociologists in spite of the fact that the mass media is so important in the modern world. The core areas for this course include: cultural levels (high, folk, and popular/mass), methods appropriate for the analysis of genres, and the importance of taste and taste cultures. I use films, recordings, slide presentations, and guest speakers. Students are given a number of options for course credit including writing social histories, sociologist as method actor, and visual analysis.

Graduate Responsibilities. I teach two graduate classes, Social Inequality, which is required for graduate students concentrating in Social Inequality and Conflict, and Sociology of Occupations, which is an elective for that same concentration.

Social Inequality. I see the course as primarily a "social stratification" course so the bulk of the material focuses on "class and caste" rather than other types of inequality. The major components include: the history of social stratification systems over time; major stratification theoretical approaches with accompanying empirical investigations; and in-depth study of a few major concepts including prestige, vertical mobility, cultural capital, and habitus. During the course, students are given the opportunity to use a selected number of research techniques fundamental to stratification research.

Sociology of Occupations. This course consists of two parts: the study of labor markets and the more traditional conceptualization of the key components of an occupation, for example, recruitment, socialization, and career. The first half of the course focuses on the new theoretical and empirical research on labor markets. Students are introduced to a broad array of sources for statistical data and tools such as those provided by the *Dictionary of Occupational Titles*. In the second half of the course, we focus on the traditional conceptualization of an occupation, and each student is required to write a final paper about one of these concepts and make copies for class members so that at the end of the quarter all students have a compendium of papers reviewing these concepts.

and undergraduate students the opportunity to take "reading courses" with faculty. If reading courses are offered, indicate some of these courses. If you have team-taught a course with someone in another department or offered cross-listed courses, note these and any other specialized offerings.

Teaching Materials: Syllabi, Handouts, Study Guides, and Examinations

The length and detail in this section is a reflection, in part, of the variety of uses for the portfolio. Currently, some departments place significant emphasis on syllabi and even attempt to evaluate them, while other institutions emphasize the utilization of high tech materials such as web pages. In this section, present a summary of the materials used in your classes. Copies of syllabi, exams, and other related materials should be provided in the appendix of the portfolio.

Teaching materials should: (a) emphasize teaching strengths and (b) explain those materials that deviate from the norm. For example, some faculty do not give dates for exams on syllabi because they aren't sure what date they will finish a particular unit. A search committee that evaluates these syllabi may consider this a significant omission. An explanation is needed. In addition, make sure your teaching materials correspond to and support your teaching philosophy and goals. For example, determine whether your exams reflect your teaching philosophy and goals, whether exams instruct, or whether they are used to fulfill a bureaucratic requirement.

Evidence of Teaching Effectiveness

Evaluating teaching effectiveness is assuming even greater importance in faculty evaluations. A number of different measures are used. Many institutions focus solely on student evaluations, but some colleges also use other measures including faculty and peer evaluations of both classroom teaching and teaching materials. This section of the portfolio should include a description of the methods used in the department, including the name of the student evaluation scale used (if there is one), peer evaluation forms, and any other documents that are used to gauge teaching effectiveness.

All of the following can be used as evidence of teaching effectiveness:

- Numerical student evaluation scores
- Written comments from students
- Faculty evaluations
- Peer evaluations of teaching (usually based on classroom observations)
- Peer evaluations of teaching materials (i.e., exams and syllabi)
- Video-taped teaching sessions
- Letters from alumni
- Teaching awards
- Letter from the department chairperson or head
- Letter from the graduate director

The style of presentation of this material is important. As a general principle, only present summations of materials in this section. You are encouraged to be creative, but not to sacrifice content for creativity. Make sure the evaluation results are clear and easy to understand and interpret. Presentation of student evaluations can be summarized in a number of different ways, including:

- **Key questions (5-point scale)**

Psy 200 Mean %	Psy 301 Mean %	Psy 256 Mean %	Psy 200 Mean %
This course contributed to my learning			
4.7 85	4.6 83	4.9 90	4.3 75
This instructor was one of the best I have had			
4.5 86	4.7 88	4.9 90	4.5 76

- **Overall, I would rate this instructor (5-point scale)**

	Econ. 201	Econ. 315	Econ. 316	Econ. 410
1990	4.1	4.5	3.9	3.1
1991	4.5	4.5	4.5	4.5
1992	4.7	4.5	4.9	4.7

Summaries often reflect average scores for a series of questions that can be compared to a benchmark value. They may also include median values as well as the percentage of the students in the class who responded to the question. Comparing class ratings over time is especially useful. The reader can note at a glance whether you were a consistent teacher, made improvements, or experienced challenges in a certain course (for effect, highlight improvements or especially high average scores).

Peer evaluations of classroom teaching can be presented the same way. Most classroom observation forms use both a numerical rating system as well as written comments. It may be best to present the numerical evaluations in summary form with, perhaps, a representative sample from the written comments, and then place copies of the forms in the appendix. For added effect, you can also include copies of comments from students in their own handwriting. You may also elect to type a representative summary of student evaluations. This option is appropriate, but may lose some of the impact associated with reading comments in the students' own handwriting. It is also very important to have faculty observe your teaching and provide written evaluations. Their feedback can be helpful in improving your teaching and their letters are a respected form of evaluation in addition to student and peer evaluations.

Don't overload this section with tables, graphs, charts, or pages of undigested data. The reader should be able to move through this section and make an assessment of how well you function in the classroom. To check for readability, ask a nonacademic or objective third party to review the information. This section is important not only to others (deans or recruitment committees) but also to you as the portfolio developer. Tracing changes in student satisfaction with certain courses over time is particularly useful. In some courses, evaluations may fluctuate rather dramatically and in other courses they may not. The time of day (8:00 a.m. vs. 12:00 p.m.), the number of students (10 vs. 100), the length of class periods (50 minutes vs. 2 hours), type of course (College Algebra vs. Advanced Calculus) should be considered; all these factors have been shown to affect student evaluations. It may be helpful to make brief explanations for fluctuations in evaluations. For example, if departmental trends show that student evaluations for introductory courses tend to be lower than those for upper division classes, or if evaluations tend to be lower for statistics classes as compared to theory courses, a brief comment regarding these patterns would be in order. In sum, an analysis of the data collected for this section can be very useful to the interested search committee. It is also acceptable to compare your numerical scores with departmental or university averages. However, avoid grandiose personal praise at the expense of others.

Evidence of Student Accomplishments

This is an important, but often neglected, area of the portfolio. This section should include a summary of accomplishments for *students who have taken your courses.* Typically, this information will reflect undergraduate accomplishments or achievements for current graduate students who took your courses as undergraduates. Students may think we are great and so may other faculty members, but evidence of student accomplishments is an important measure of effectiveness. What follows is a partial list of material that may be included in this section:

- Student presentations and publications
- Student awards
- Admissions to graduate schools
- Successful employment of students, particularly if related to training in your courses
- Representative examples of student work, such as term papers or data analysis

Present summaries of the materials in the body of the portfolio and reproduce the materials in an appendix. For example, you might write, "Over the past four years, seven students under my instruction presented papers at undergraduate sessions at professional meetings or departmental or campus-wide symposiums and three have published articles from term papers or projects that I directed."

Teaching-Related Activities

The purpose of this section is to document all the activities you engaged in that involve teaching. Once again, the range of information relevant to this section is broad and may include:

- Advisement
- Workshops attended and led
- Publications on teaching
- Paper presentations
- Leadership of or participation in special programs, internships, or fellowships
- Teaching-related offices and committee work in professional organizations

It is appropriate to list some presentations, papers, and publications in this section that are also listed on your vita under professional development. That is perfectly acceptable; the purpose of the portfolio is to identify teaching accomplishments, and all relevant material is important. This section may also include material on specific efforts you made to improve your teaching. Perhaps you partnered with a colleague to monitor each other's classroom teaching, conducted an experiment on the effectiveness of different teaching styles on classroom outcomes, or taught via Web-CT. Such experiences suggest a willingness to try new approaches to improve your teaching.

Future Teaching Goals and Plans

First, identify the time frame for future plans (e.g., a five-year time frame that includes yearly updates). Second, goals and plans should have an objective, measurable component and be justified based on course objectives. An informal "management by objective" approach allows you to formalize goals and evaluate outcomes. For example, higher education is involved in a technological revolution. One of your goals may be to start interactive teaching, develop a web site, or create a CD-ROM. Be imaginative. For example, I know of a graduate student who set up a web site and interacts with his students via the site; a faculty member took a course in how to be a standup comic and uses what he learned to teach his classes. Another instructor took her students to a Grateful Dead concert and another faculty member took a group of students to visit the Sister Spirit Commune in Mississippi, both to examine countercultures. Here is an opportunity to add an exciting new dimension to teaching. Be *bold!*

Curriculum Vita

A curriculum vita should be included in this section. Information about vita development is provided in Chapter 4. However, several comments relative to its relationship to the teaching portfolio are in order. Remember, information provided in the vita should support and reinforce the teaching portfolio. For completeness sake, also remember that a vita should be included in the teaching portfolio even if it has been provided during an earlier phase of the application process.

Appendices

Any additional material you believe is pertinent to your application packet can be included in this section. The material in this section should be referenced in the body of the teaching portfolio. Be sure to provide legible copies that are clearly identified with titles and directly associated with specific portfolio sections.

Final Reflections

Each candidate's teaching portfolio will be (and should be) his or her own creation. Also remember that certain portions of this chapter will not be applicable to graduate students about to enter the employment market as compared to individuals who are re-entering the market. Develop your portfolio accordingly. It will take time to compile a solid portfolio, and you may wonder whether it is worth the effort. Try to remember that, aside from being a vital piece of your application packet, the portfolio provides a vehicle for reflection. Most of us (academics in general, educators in particular) are striving to identify the essence of "good teaching"—and to apply those principles as we teach. However, we can all improve. Developing a teaching portfolio will help you work toward excellence in the classroom.

Most of the experts on portfolios stress the need for faculty collegiality and trust. Faculty and graduate students submit papers for review by peer referees, but we are often hesitant to invite anyone into our classrooms. Portfolios will only be useful in improving teaching if they are developed and used honestly. When you take the time and effort to develop a teaching portfolio, it shows that you are interested in building a culture of teaching collegiality and trust that will benefit both the prospective department and students you will instruct in the future.

6

The Interview Process

It is during interviews that faculty members, search committees, and candidates interact face to face. Up until this point, candidates have been faceless people whose application packets have served to establish their worth and credibility. While this presentation on paper is sufficient to narrow the search, it is the actual interview that is the deciding factor. Many candidates have stellar application packets, but do not fair well during an interview. In contrast, a candidate may not have been considered the number one choice for the position but interviewed well and is able to convince department members that he or she is the best fit. Note that this does not mean that candidates with unacceptable application information are likely to get a job because they interview well. To the contrary, such candidates typically do not make the final cut of onsite candidates. What this does suggest is that being able to interview well will help to distinguish you from the "short" list of other candidates. This chapter focuses on successfully interviewing in a variety of settings and practical hints to make the process easier and more effective.

■ Interviewing at Conferences and Meetings

To expedite the search process and save time and expenses, many institutions schedule preliminary "mini interviews" during national and regional conferences (sometimes these interviews take place before application packets are due). This allows faculty members to meet a large number of potential candidates in a structured setting. Such interviews also allow you to interact with a wide variety of representatives in your field. Taking part in preliminary interviews provides an excellent opportunity to develop and enhance your interviewing skills. Some graduate students may question the importance of taking part in the conference interview process and feel that it would be a waste of time. However, these interviews can be important introductory sessions between you and prospective institutions. Remember, in most instances, faculty members have not met you and have only briefly reviewed your profile on paper. Thus these initial interviews enable them to put a name and profile with a face and personality. Yes, conference interviews often serve as "weeding out" venues for some institutions. But they can also enable you as a graduate student to identify potentially viable institutions you had not really considered before and to note those that are obviously an ill-fit for your background and research and teaching interests. Once a visual link has been formed between you and faculty members from prospective institutions, you can build on this initial interaction (they are also more likely to remember you when they return to campus and begin developing their list of the most viable candidates). And if you are already attending a discipline conference, why not take advantage of the opportunity to interview?

Note that these settings can be quite off-putting for some (i.e., interviews in crowded rooms, strictly timed sessions, bells, open sessions, white noise, numerous interviews in relatively short time periods). However, those candidates who are able to get beyond the challenges may be better prepared for lengthier onsite interviews. While job offers are rarely made during such interviews, you can develop skills that will be invaluable on the job market, and spark the attention of faculty at institutions that interest you. The following suggestions will help maximize mini-conference interviews.

Before the Conference Interview

Expect to spend some conference sessions interviewing or preparing to interview. It is often difficult to take full advantage of interviews when you are busy during the conference. It may be best to minimize actual conference presentations so that you can focus sufficient time on interviewing. Spend some time thinking about possible responses. Be able to clearly and briefly state your research project and objectives. Practice responses to standard questions so that you appear calm and confident (e.g., What are your research interests? Why are you interested in XYZ institution? Describe your dissertation/research results. What classes can you or would you like to teach?). Certain material is also expected. Bring at least twenty copies of your vita (most conference hotels have copy machines if necessary) and take a few complete interview packets (writing samples, evaluations, and teaching statement). Most interviewers won't ask for this documentation but, if someone does, you appear prepared by having it. Last, bring business cards (make sure your cards include your e-mail address and cellular phone number). It is also important to wear professional attire. This means a business suit, business dress, or slacks and a sport jacket. Make sure your clothes are pressed and crisp (no gym shoes!). It is not necessary to bring a large wardrobe, but rather several items that can be interchanged for different professional "looks."

During the Conference Interview

Check your interview mailbox at least every one to two hours. Most structured conference interviews update candidates about interested institutions and often preschedule interviews. In most cases, it is your responsibility to monitor your mail for interview information. Don't be afraid to ask for an interview. If you learn that representatives from a certain school will be onsite, attempt to make contact and set up a mini-interview. This shows your level of interest and determination to talk with them. Arrive early to get your thoughts and documents in order and to help calm potential nervousness. Although it may be challenging, try to enjoy the process. Consider conference and meeting interviews an opportunity to meet faculty members from many schools, meet other candidates on the job market, and practice. Maintaining the proper perspective can make the experience more enjoyable and foster a positive attitude. While interviewers are looking for a candidate who will fit departmental needs, they are also interested in one who has a pleasing disposition and demeanor. Take the process seriously, but don't take the process *too* seriously. For most schools this is an initial screening process.

Take notes during the actual interview (names, interests, key points about the institution) so that you can refer to this information in subsequent correspondence. Also, prepare several interesting questions for the interviewers (feel free to use the same questions for each). For example, What are the departmental foci? Is there a methodological focus in the department? Describe the academic profile of students. Teaching loads. Departmental labs. Ask questions about the institution. This information will help you determine whether you are a fit for the post and also show that you are interested and excited about the institution. It is important to remember that the interview is also a chance to learn about the institution. At the end of the interview, ask for the interviewer's business card. This shows your interest and provides you with contact information. It is often helpful to write short notes about the person and the interview on the back of the card.

Although most mini-interviews will take place in a predesignated place, also prepare for nontraditional interviews. Faculty members may have a variety of tasks during a conference that preclude the traditional interview setup. Thus, interviews can take place over coffee, in a hotel lobby or lounge, or during lunch between sessions. Although it may not appear to be, it is still an interview. And be aware that you are often "interviewing" even outside of the formal process. Remember, faculty frequent hotel and neighborhood restaurants, coffee shops, and stores. It is not uncommon to see people in conference sessions, on elevators, or in hotel lobbies. Therefore, being at your professional best is essential.

After the Conference Interview

Send a brief thank you by e-mail to the representatives with whom you interviewed from each school. Even if you realize an institution is not a good fit, it is still important that they remember you in a positive way (who knows, you may seek employment there in the future). However, send a more detailed thank you note or e-mail to those schools that really interest you, expressing your excitement about potentially interviewing on campus for a position. In the correspondence, mention something about the interview and yourself that will jog their memories and also make reference to key points from the conversation. Based on time constraints and logistics, you may not have been able to interview with every institution that was interested in speaking with you (or vice versa). Send a letter of interest and vita to those schools with whom you were unable to interview.

▇ Telephone Interviews

Telephone interviews are another approach used to narrow the job search. They are quite popular among departments with limited search budgets who wish to have some personal interaction with potential candidates before the short list is determined. Telephone interviews are often 45 minutes to one hour in length and provide the search committee with an opportunity to talk with candidates in detail about their application information. Expect the same types of questions listed in the previous section on conference interviewing (and in the onsite interview section below), be prepared to ask several questions, and research the institution and department to familiarize yourself with its major specialties and department faculty members. Have a copy of any correspondence you provided (cover letter, vita, and writing samples) at your disposal to promptly and succinctly answer questions. Have a pen and paper nearby to jot notes and questions. Be sure to schedule the interview at a location and time when you will not be interrupted, disengage call-waiting on your telephone, and make sure you are comfortable. Although seemingly less formal, such interviews should be taken seriously because the search committee is typically trying to make a decision about which candidates from a longer list should be eliminated and which ones should be offered an onsite interview. Try to be especially articulate during telephone interviews and speak with confidence since you must make a good impression orally to show that you are the best candidate for the position. This is often challenging simply because of the medium being used.

■ Onsite Interviews and the "Job Talk"

If you have reached this point, it means that the search committee is impressed with your application packet and you have made the short list. It is now time to compete directly with a small, select pool of candidates for the position. In this book I make a distinction between the onsite interview and the "job talk." The former represents all the activities that take place upon a candidate's arrival until he/she leaves the presence of faculty members at the interested institution, while the latter refers specifically to the academic presentation made during the onsite interview. Thus the onsite interview includes the job talk as well as one-on-one faculty interviews, interviews with graduate students, meals with faculty, and teaching a class. And although I make this distinction, in some circles, the onsite interview and job talk are used interchangeably.

Typically a representative from the committee or a departmental assistant will make travel arrangements for you. Some colleges require candidates to make and pay for their own flights and then reimburse them upon arrival or by mail. This process instills a certain level of accountability on the part of each candidate and also helps ensure that he or she will attend the interview. (Note: This option may be financially constraining for graduate students on fixed incomes. If it poses a problem, simply request that the institution make the flight arrangements and state the reasons why. If they cannot comply, ask whether they can guarantee that reimbursement will occur at the interview.)

The outcome of the onsite interview process will determine who is offered the position. Needless to say, the interview is the most important element in the entire application process. Candidates are brought in to talk about themselves, their research interests, and experiences and show that they are the best fit for the position. As mentioned in earlier chapters, the search committee and other department members are looking for someone who is best professionally and personally. It is your challenge to convince them that you are that person. And while some aspects of the interview process will be beyond your control and there are no guarantees of selection, certain strategies can be used to help make the experience a positive one and increase the likelihood of a favorable outcome. Onsite interviews are discussed broadly here and each component detailed in subsequent sections.

Initial Preparation

• *Let your dissertation committee and classmates critique your scholarly presentation (i.e., the job talk presentation).* This is crucial! Ask them to raise critical, difficult questions so that you can practice responding. They will also give you feedback to improve your responses. After these mock presentations, develop a list of the types of questions you might expect and then write down appropriate answers. Although you cannot think of all such questions, this exercise will help prepare you for the inevitable onslaught during the interview. Videotape yourself during a mock job talk, presentation, or practice teaching presentations. Also time yourself because most interviews allow between 45 minutes to one hour for the formal presentation. It is important to stay within the prescribed time limit. Practice, practice, practice (again)!! Remember that after your job talk has been fine tuned, it can be revamped for varied settings. Find out who will be in attendance at the presentation (e.g., only faculty members, people from other departments, deans, the provost). Also be prepared to present based on a broad topic related to your area as provided by the interested department. (Refer to a suggested outline later in this chapter.)

• *Ask if you will be expected to teach a class.* If possible, focus on some aspect of your dissertation. This will reinforce your research interests to search committee members who may be in attendance and also minimize the amount of up-front preparation you must make. However, it is common to be given a lecture topic. Confirm the class size and adjust the presentation for the class level. (Refer to a suggested outline later in this chapter.)

• *Review the web site of the prospective school.* Determine some of the research interests of the department members, the school's objectives, and the department's focus. Develop questions for faculty members based on their areas of interest. While this can be time consuming, it is impressive because it shows people that you took the time to research the institution and their interests.

   • *Find out where you are in the process.* Are you the first or last candidate? How long is the short list? When will decisions be made? Most institutions will be forthcoming with as much information as is available.

   • *Carry your presentation material with you in a briefcase or carryon during the flight, train, or bus trip.* Avoid placing items such as overheads, slides, handouts, and disks needed during the interview in your checked luggage. They may become lost or delayed and, without them, your interview may be severely undermined (wear a professional outfit on the outbound trip for the same reason).

   • *If you are ABD, continue to work toward graduating—this is the objective.* Avoid letting the excitement and planning for an interview divert your attention from your primary goal. Maintain balance. Also be sure your adviser's letter of recommendation includes your projected completion date and coincides with what you will provide during the interview. Have a graduation strategy. It may not always be ideal to graduate one semester and begin a position the next. Try to time your graduation to maximize your options. In some cases, it is best to begin interviews in the fall for positions the following fall. Another option would be to finish in December of an academic year, but apply for jobs that begin the following fall. This will give you ample time to apply for positions, convert the dissertation into articles or a monograph, rest, start additional publications, develop courses, and make arrangements if you must relocate.

Logistics

   • *If possible, schedule to arrive the day before.* This will enable you to be rested and prevent travel delays from affecting the interview schedule.

   • *Ask if your teaching and/or dissertation presentations can take place early in the day so that you will be at your best.* Most people become drained as the day progresses. It may be difficult to give your best presentation at 4:00 p.m. after almost eight hours of mini-interviews with faculty members. Realize that some institutions may not be able to accommodate this request due to scheduling difficulties with faculty and deans, but it does not hurt to ask. Request at least thirty minutes free time *prior* to presentations to collect your thoughts, locate and review handouts and overheads, and to relax. Avoid leaving an interview session and immediately making a presentation. You may not have sufficient time to "re-group."

• *Provide handouts during your presentations (both during academic talks and teaching presentations).* This highlights your writing skills and can be used to include topics that cannot be discussed due to time constraints. Handouts also provide people with something tangible to later associate with your presentation. Some people avoid using handouts because they believe the audience will focus on the handouts rather than the presentation. This potential problem can be addressed by keeping handouts to a minimum and only distributing them at the specific period in your presentation when they will be referenced. Also decide which technology you will be using (e.g., PowerPoint) and then prepare several backup options (overheads and hardcopies). Last, anticipate and be prepared to answer certain questions both for faculty and student-focused audiences (e.g., your methodology, controversial elements of your study, its contribution to the discipline, justifications for certain techniques).

• *Take some high-energy snacks to pep you up midday.* Carry with you breath freshener, toothbrush, floss, a small container of spot remover, and any medication you need. Also eat light during lunch to prevent becoming sleepy.

• *Expect a lengthy interview process over a one to two day period.* These may include a series of short interviews with faculty members and school officials, a lunch interview, and a dinner interview, among others.

During the Interview

• *Be prepared for a variety of questions regarding your teaching and/or research agendas.* Be able to suggest new courses that you could develop and teach. Also be prepared to quickly list the types of books and articles you might use in an existing or new course. Have several "smart" questions to pose to interviewers (e.g., regarding creative methods or ways to advance the literature in your field). Develop different questions for different groups of people (junior faculty, senior faculty, department chair or head, dean) or for different types of institutions (e.g., teaching rather than research institutions). Note that you may be able to use the same or similar questions at each onsite interview. If you are ABD, you will be asked about your anticipated dissertation completion date. You may have to convince the department of the timely completion of your dissertation. Be prepared to discuss exactly where you are in the writing process.

• *Be honest and avoid being a "yes" person.* You want to get the best job, but you also want the selection process to be a "win/win" situation for you and the institution. Don't make promises you cannot keep. This will only create problems if you are selected and begin your career there. While it is important to get a job, it is equally important to be able to keep it and be successful at it. So although you may be tempted to answer "yes" to every question about your ability to teach certain courses, mentor students, or provide certain skills to the department or program, this is not good practice. Be able to present your skills and assets (for example, if you anticipate a question about your ability to teach a course, prepare a syllabus and provide it to the search committee), but be careful not to embellish so that the institution will eventually be disappointed when you cannot deliver on promises made during your interview or you are unable to perform the necessary roles to obtain tenure.

• *Watch and listen.* Try to get some sense of the area, campus, and the department. Is this a place where you would feel comfortable and happy? Do you think your research interests would be appreciated and supported? Are faculty and staff friendly? Professional? Do department members seem collegial with each other? Ask questions as well. Make sure you talk with recent appointees (new assistant professors, people one to two years out of graduate school). Get their opinion about the institution, the department, and their transition experience. Find out what suggestions they have for new candidates on the market. Can you see yourself living in the area? Ask them to schedule a tour of the local area to show your interest in relocating. Given the importance of the interview, it is easy to focus on impressing the institution members and fail to critically evaluate the institution and area from your perspective. More information on this subject is provided in Chapter 8.

After the Interview

Send thank you letters, cards, or e-mails immediately after the onsite interview (make sure you get contact information from each person with whom you speak).

Go on as many onsite interviews for appropriate positions in your research/teaching areas as possible. However, do not interview at institutions in which you have no interest. This is a waste of their time and resources as well as your own.

Developing the Academic Job Talk Presentation

The caliber of your academic job talk will greatly influence your standing and ranking as a candidate. This presentation should be used to showcase your research project, skills as a researcher and presenter, ability to answer questions extemporaneously, and your savvy and professionalism under pressure. No matter how impressive you have been during one-on-one interviews, a poorly executed job talk can greatly reduce your chances of selection for the position. Again, be sure to give yourself sufficient time to develop the presentation, ask for advice and suggestions from departmental mentors and your dissertation committee chairperson, and tailor the presentation to the specific guidelines provided by the prospective department (i.e., time limits, usually 30–45 minutes for the presentation, followed by a 15–30 minute Question and Answer [Q&A] session). Most departments will be relatively open in terms of the format—this will enable you to develop a presentation that is informative, focused, and that highlights you as the ideal candidate. Be sure to consider presentation dictates in your respective disciplines. For example, some institutions may expect you to speak extemporaneously and stand during the talk, while others find actually reading your work verbatim from a seated position appropriate (I personally find the latter type of presentation somewhat stilted and boring and do not recommend it). No matter the approach you use, be sure to engage the audience. As a test of your ability to explain the primary facets of your research, be able to provide a 1-minute, 5-minute, and 45-minute summary of your research (this skill will come in handy during various phases of your search). In addition to the above strategies to consider during the on-campus visit (especially practicing your presentations to stay within the expected time constraints and providing appropriate handouts), the following outline may be helpful when organizing and preparing for the academic job talk. Be sure that the job talk addresses who, what, where, when, why, and how relative to your research and clearly illustrates your skills and competence. The format below may vary based on your discipline or methodology, but in general an academic job talk presentation should include the following components (you will note that the presentation flows in a manner similar to an academic research paper):

1. *An informative title.* Include the title, your name, institution, and date on any handouts, overheads, or visual presentation. The presentation title should summarize the research.

2. *Research purpose.* A broad statement that summarizes the project.

3. *Significance of the research.* Link the study to the larger body of research in your discipline and explain the limitation(s) it is addressing.

4. *Theory or theoretical framework.* Briefly reference the theory on which the research is grounded and several of the key scholars. If you cannot go into detail about this information, mention that you would be happy to provide additional information during the Q&A session at the end of the presentation.

5. *Research questions.* Succinctly present the research questions and how they are informed by the literature and selected theory. If appropriate, present the hypotheses and/or research propositions.

6. *Data and methods.* Clearly discuss the data and methods used and justify their use. Mention any major limitations and associated implications for your research.

7. *Major findings.* Present major results, any atypical or

unexpected findings, and revisit the research questions. If you are still completing the project, present preliminary findings or mention anticipated ones.

8. *Summary.* Briefly summarize your results.

9. *Links to broader issues.* Provide several connections between your work and existing research, social policy, or broader themes in the discipline.

10. *Future research.* Briefly comment on your future research interests as they relate to the project. If you are ABD, remind the audience of your expected completion date.

11. *Conclusion.* Provide brief concluding remarks about the research, its importance, and expected benefits to the discipline.

Teaching a Class

It is not uncommon for candidates to be asked to teach a class. Some committees may feel that job talks are over-rehearsed and do not provide a true reflection of your presentation skills and teaching abilities. Others *expect* you to interact well with other academics, but are also interested in how you interact with undergraduate and graduate students in the program and answer their questions. Still other institutions require an academic presentation and class presentation to provide several venues for faculty members from a large, busy department to evaluate you. Teaching institutions will be specifically interested in your ability to successfully instruct a class and how you interact with students. Regardless of the reason, this portion of the interview process should be taken as seriously as the formal academic presentation. Students in class will be asked to evaluate you and their opinions are given some credence when final decisions are made.

In preparation for a class presentation, have a conversation with your contact person about logistics. Determine the approximate number of students in the course, their background relative to your topic, overall classifications in school, whether most students are majors or whether they are taking the course as an elective. Also find out the amount of time you will have and the desired format (e.g., a 30-minute teaching presentation followed by a 30-minute Q&A). Answers to these questions will help you develop a presentation best suited for the class level (be sure to adhere to the time allotments). When you arrive, ask to see the classroom before your presentation so that you can get acclimated. Request equipment (e.g., PowerPoint, overhead projector, copies, dry-erase board, a laptop linked to a USB projector or a computer with flash drive capability) in advance and ask for at least 15 minutes preparation time before the class begins.

Attempt to present the material in an engaging, interesting format (e.g., a game format or challenging introductory questions). Consider using an interactive learning activity if the class will include fewer than forty students. This is especially important if your research is quantitative in nature or highly theoretical or if the class consists of freshmen and sophomores or students with little or no knowledge of the subject area. During one of my job talks I was asked to present my research on regression and cluster analysis to a class of undergraduate students (most of whom were taking the course as an elective). After much concern about the best way to present somewhat dense information, I opted to develop scenarios in which the class had to "predict" the outcome. We then determined how accurate their predictions had been. This format created a good transition into the remainder of the presentation and served to hold their interest. Last, provide a handout that summarizes your talk. Remember to develop the presentation for a student audience. It should be academic, but not as academically detailed as the job talk. The following outline may help you organize a teaching presentation:

1. *An informative, engaging title.* Include the title, your name, institution, and date on any handouts, overheads, or visual presentation. The presentation title should summarize the teaching subject and illicit excitement and interest from students.

2. *Subject's importance.* Briefly explain why the subject is important and why you are qualified to teach it. Also link the subject, if appropriate, to your research and teaching interests.

3. *Define key concepts.* Provide concise, thoughtful definitions for key concepts to be referenced during the presentation. Explain why the concepts are important and inform students that you will be re-visiting these concepts.

4. *Stimulate discussion and interest.* Play an introductory game, use visual aides, begin with a short, creative Q&A or dis-

cussion. Such activities will engage students and draw them into the experience. It is best to capture their attention early in the presentation because it is often difficult to recapture it if students have disengaged because the initial minutes of the class are uninteresting.

5. *Lecture/discussion.* The actual information to be taught should be presented during this period. You should have a specific amount of information you wish to convey and be intentional about the points you would like the students to remember. This portion of the presentation should be timely (about 20 minutes), informative, and reinforced using either a handout or some other type of visual aid. Be sure that the presentation addresses who, what, where, when, why, and how relative to the subject.

6. *Summary and conclusion.* Briefly re-visit the key issues presented and remind students of other related issues. If appropriate, provide practical connections between the subject and their experiences as students, young citizens, and productive members of society.

Sample Interview Questions

The following types of questions should be addressed during the onsite interview. It is important to get a response from the chairperson/head of the department and also to get opinions from a variety of people with whom you interview. Look for consistency in responses as well as candor.

Department issues. You may be somewhat hesitant to ask specific questions about the ideology, environment, and expectations in a prospective department for fear of appearing suspicious, anxious, or overly concerned. But remember, if an offer is made and you accept, the department will become your place of employment and its members will be your colleagues. So it is crucial to get as much information as possible about the department. Refer to the departmental web page to ascertain facts such as the departmental mix in terms of assistant, associate, and full professors and to determine whether the department is demographically diverse in terms of women, people of color, and faculty experience. Also, interviewers expect candidates to ask questions and your ability to do so suggests a desire to make an informed decision and the ability to engage in critical inquiry. If you are visiting a smaller institution where you will also be interviewing with faculty outside your prospective department, still feel comfortable posing broad questions about the institutional environment and their experiences.

1. *Does the department have a theoretical focus?* That is, postmodern, postcolonialism, Marxist, classical, or a combination? Does the department have a methodological focus (qualitative research, quantitative research, a mixture)?

2. *What is the annual review process?* How are research and teaching progress assessed? Is there a departmental evaluative rubric? Is there a formal mentoring process for junior faculty?

3. *What is the department's tenure and/or promotion track record, at the levels of both associate and full professor?* What was the academic profile of the last tenured faculty member? What are the components of the tenure equation and their expected mix (research, teaching, and service)? Does the process stress research more than teaching or vice versa? How is tenure specifically determined? Do associate and full professors make tenure decisions or are such decisions made solely by full professors? What is the retention rate for new faculty? Attrition rate? Do most faculty members make careers in the department?

4. *If the department is not demographically diverse in terms of women, people of color, and faculty experience, are there plans to increase diversity?* How? Is the campus diverse?

5. *Do faculty collaborate on research? Faculty and graduate students?* Is the environment conducive to this type of exchange? If desired, are their possibilities for administrative responsibilities?

6. *What is the department's vision?* Plans for the future? Growth potential? What is your perception of the department's reputation and position of importance within the overall institution?

Junior faculty roles and responsibilities. Be comfortable asking questions about the responsibilities of junior faculty, in general, and relative to the prospective position, in particular. It will be important to understand protocol and the working environment, short- and long-term expectations, and mechanisms that are in place to facilitate a smooth transition for junior faculty. Here are a few questions to consider:

1. *Is a reduced teaching schedule an option for the first year (to allow time to develop courses and/or to establish a research agenda)?* Is it possible to buy out of a course during a semester? Are research sabbaticals or research leaves available?

2. *Describe the research expectations for junior faculty during years one and two (in general).* Describe the teaching responsibilities for junior faculty during years one and two (in general).

3. *Describe the committee responsibilities for a typical junior faculty member during years one and two.* Describe mentoring responsibilities for junior faculty during years one and two. When are junior faculty expected to serve on master's theses and Ph.D. committees?

4. *Describe the tenure process.* Do existing publications count toward tenure? Are certain publications considered more heavily than others? If so, what is the hierarchy?

Meeting Department Members

During the on-campus interview, expect to meet with most, if not all, of the members of a department and/or program. These mini-interviews may be one-on-one sessions or with groups of colleagues. They may be quite formal or take place during meals and departmental gatherings. However, even when the setting is less formal (e.g., a lunch interview) be mindful that the session is still part of the overall interview process. Meeting department members provides potential colleagues with the opportunity to determine whether you are a good fit professionally and personally (also refer to the section in Chapter 4 on the ideal candidate), ask specific questions about your research and teaching, and also determine the possibility for research collaboration and/or co-teaching. These interviews also provide you with an opportunity to get a feel for people who may become your colleagues and peers. And just as they are assessing your merit, ask questions of them, note how they interact with each other, and try to determine whether you would enjoy working with them.

Be prepared to interact with a variety of people. Just as there is diversity at any place of employment, you may meet the occasional curmudgeon, rising star, patriarch, matriarch, activist, introvert, and other associated people (I think one of the strengths of academia is its creative, often eccentric members). And although you may differ from some of your potential colleagues in many ways, the important point of commonality is the academic endeavor—and this common goal can be the source of many interesting conversations during your interview. Most important, be prepared to answer a myriad of questions and be comfortable asking specific questions about the department. After each interview, remember to ask for a business card so that you can send a note or e-mail to department members thanking them for their time.

Reflections After the Onsite Interview

After each onsite interview, objectively assess your performance. Did the interview go smoothly? If not, what were the rough areas? What should be improved about the academic presentation, teaching the class, or interviews with faculty? Did the handouts enhance the presentation? Were there timing issues? Were you unable to answer specific questions during the formal presentation completely or to your satisfaction? Reevaluate each component of the interview so that improvements can be made for subsequent interviews.

■ Diplomacy When Interviewing

Although it will probably not occur, be prepared for unexpected, inappropriate comments by people during interviews. It is important to know how to handle such situations with diplomacy and professionalism. Should topics arise that are inappropriate and potentially negative (e.g., a faculty member mentions departmental factions and wishes to gauge where you might side on a particular issue, or a faculty member begins to disparage a departmental colleague or academic in the discipline), do not enter into a negative conversation during the discussion (no matter what others are doing or saying). Attempt to graciously return the conversation to the interview at hand by referencing another subject or asking the faculty member a question about his/her research. For example, if a faculty member wishes to gauge your views about departmental politics, a comment such as, "I believe that some of the strengths of a career in academia are the diverse methodological, theoretical, and political stances professors bring to the research and teaching endeavor. I look forward to that diversity," should defuse the situation. Or if asked about a topic that seems inappropriate, simply state, "I'm not familiar with that issue, so I can't comment," smile, and continue to graciously ask a question about another subject. Or if a negative comment is made about an individual in your discipline or department and the speaker seems to be waiting for you to respond, you could simply state, "That has not been my experience with Dr. Jobes, but I am very interested in *your experiences* gathering data in Eastern Asia. I've been looking forward to chatting with you about them." Again, asking a question about the research and/or teaching interests of the other person will usually change the subject.

Also be aware that questions regarding your religion, marital status, age, sexual orientation, spouse's occupation, or children (existing or planned) are illegal. They should not be posed. However, if they are, use the above noted types of techniques to divert the conversation. Based on the gravity of the experience and those involved, this may be a red flag that the institution may not be a positive place to begin your career. You should be cognizant of subjects and questions to avoid as well. In general, avoid asking personal questions, introducing potentially controversial subjects in a conversation (such as religion, sex, politics), or discussing issues that are debatable. Because you do not know the personal politics, belief systems, or lifestyles of faculty members, you may unknowingly offend someone and undermine your potential as a viable candidate. Remember that department politics and varied personalities and temperaments will exist at all institutions. Your interview objective is to interact as positively as possible with each person you meet and avoid alienating or offending people. Developing diplomacy skills will serve you well.

■ Self-Presentation: Social Skills and Attire

No matter how impressive your research or how great you look on paper, how you present yourself during the onsite interview can make or break your chances of being selected for a position. I address issues of appearance later in this same section; however, social and communication skills are often noticed as readily as appearance. A candidate with a strong academic profile who also has a positive personality and exudes a team-oriented attitude will probably be considered a better fit for the position than one who has a strong profile but who cannot communicate effectively during the job talk, makes offensive or defensive statements during lunch, is argumentative during the Q&A session, or is condescending to students during the teaching presentation. Remember, you are competing with other candidates and your professional and personal demeanor will be evaluated. Certain issues relative to effective communication can be addressed more easily than others. For example, practicing your job talk and teaching presentations numerous times will enable you to speak confidently, clearly, and with ease (even if you are somewhat nervous). Preparing possible responses to anticipated questions regarding your research will help as well. However, other social skills may require more intentionality on your part (especially if you have spent the last three years collecting and analyzing data in relative isolation and have forgotten certain social graces).

Although I provide a list below of common mistakes to avoid during an interview, several broad issues should be considered. In general, you should endeavor to show members of prospective departments that you are the best professional and personal fit. Your research and teaching experiences and onsite presentations will help illustrate the former; your social skills during the interview period will confirm the latter. It is important to be confident without being cocky, assertive without being confrontational, and approachable without being unduly informal. This may seem like a difficult balancing act, but it requires being aware of your strengths and growth areas. For example, because of the time and energy expended doing graduate research, it is easy to become overly sensitive regarding your research. Being cognizant of this tendency can prevent you from becoming easily offended by seemingly "obtuse" questions, people who are not as impressed by your work as you are, and people who may question the contribution of your research to the discipline. Exhibiting appropriate social skills also means avoiding a diva mentality regarding your potential (i.e., avoid saying that you are an "expert" or "scholar" in your discipline—that is a comment others should make about you). Even if your research has revolutionized the understanding of a certain topic in your discipline, a little humility still goes a long way. Interestingly, although academia often rewards people for individualistic behavior (e.g., publishing sole-authored books and articles), in general, faculty are expected to be team-oriented.

Also be sure to be attentive to the varied people and groups you meet during an onsite interview. I remember an instance during graduate school when a candidate for an assistant professor position was quite impressive when interacting with the faculty. However, during the meeting with us graduate students, he opened a newspaper and began to read. He did not consider interacting with graduate students important. Needless to say, his actions eliminated him as a candidate for the post. In general, faculty members are interested in a candidate who is collegial. Here are seven other common mistakes to avoid during an interview.

1. *Avoid making disparaging remarks (in general).* Even if your comments are about someone unknown to faculty, negative remarks may suggest a lack of professionalism and potential mean spiritedness.

2. *Avoid gossip.* Even if people who are interviewing you become informal and begin to gossip, simply smile, but don't join the conversation. Again, asking a professional question can do wonders to change the conversation.

3. *Know when to listen and when to speak.* Although you are probably excited about the opportunity to share your research with whoever will listen, note whether you are dominating a conversation. Although you are expected to speak prolifically about your specific project during the actual job talk presentation, be sure to *engage* in conversations (i.e., two-way and group dialogue) during interview sessions, lunch and dinner gatherings, and group sessions. Remember to research faculty areas of teaching and research interests and refer to this information to stimulate conver-

sations. The faculty want to know that you can communicate effectively and that you are knowledgeable about certain subject matter, but avoid suggesting that you are self-absorbed. In addition, giving others an opportunity to speak will enable you to get to know them.

4. *Intentionally select meals.* During meals, avoid ordering items that are potentially messy or greasy (e.g., foods in barbecue sauce) or things that could get stuck in your teeth (such as spinach). If you are asked to order first, merely say, "Oh, why don't you order, I just need a few more minutes to decide." The choices made by faculty will inform you about how to order (i.e., the price range, whether appetizers will be ordered, whether a full meal or just sandwiches are expected) and whether the meal will be lengthy or a quick bite.

5. *Avoid alcoholic beverages.* Certain books on interviewing suggest that it is best to follow the dictates of the group when alcohol is concerned and that people may be offended if they order alcoholic beverages and you don't. I disagree. I suggest that interviewees avoid alcohol because of its potentially negative effects on good judgment and discretion. Being sober will decrease the chances of a faux pas. And because it is now more common for people to avoid alcoholic beverages for reasons such as health and religion, your decision not to drink should not be offensive.

6. *Never forget you are being interviewed.* If the interview is going well, there is a tendency to become too informal—especially during events such as lunch, dinner, or during automobile drives from one site to another. Remember that you are being interviewed from the moment you meet a faculty member from the prospective institution (i.e., if someone picks you up at the airport) until you leave (i.e., you are no longer in the presence of faculty members). Many blunders have been made during a particularly lively dinner or as a candidate was being driven back to the airport.

7. *Avoid condescending verbiage.* Be mindful of words that may be offensive to listeners. Also remember that during an interview you will most likely meet people from different backgrounds, religions, cultures, lifestyles—and academic perspectives! For example, comments such as "it is obvious to the

trained scholar," "clearly my findings," or "the quantitative nature of my research is more rigorous than qualitative approaches" should be avoided. Furthermore, comments about "those people," disdainful remarks about ill-prepared undergraduate students you have taught, and references to "clearly flagrant flaws" in the research of a particular scholar may be viewed negatively by faculty members.

Although you want to avoid putting your foot in your mouth, you should not become so guarded that it prevents you from being accessible or results in disingenuous behavior. It is important to be yourself. Unsure about whether certain personal habits or behavior are socially unacceptable? Ask a close friend, partner, or a member of your dissertation committee if they have noticed any comments or behavior of yours that might be considered unprofessional or that might undermine a successful interview—and make changes accordingly.

During an interview, it is also important to look professional and polished. Business attire is generally expected during the actual interview and job talk presentation (no blue jeans). Business casual attire may be appropriate for more informal phases of the interview (dinner, a gathering at the home of a faculty member), but be sure to ask your campus contact person or the search committee chairperson about the dress protocol first. Because interviews can be somewhat stressful, be comfortably dressed in clothes that are relaxing and appealing. When in doubt, stick with comfort (a job talk may not be the time to try out new shoes or a new suit). Your clothing should enhance your presentation and not detract from it. When faculty members interact with you, their attention and focus should be drawn to the content of the presentation or the conversation and not your attire. Too much jewelry or make-up, noisy jewelry, wrinkled clothes, overly distracting ties, and unkempt hair are examples of potentially distracting items of which you should be aware. If you have multiple body piercings and tattoos, decisions should be made regarding whether to wear clothing that covers tattoos and whether you should limit the number of pierced jewelry worn. Bring several changes of clothing to an interview. In order to minimize the amount of clothing needed, items should complement each other and be interchangeable as well.

It may be best to travel light so that you do not have to check your luggage. I know of a situation when a candidate's luggage, including presentation material, was misplaced on a flight. Although the candidate was apologetic and the department members were more than understanding, the interview did not go well and the candidate was not selected for the position. This strategy will prevent such incidents.

■ Handling Employment Offers

After you've been made a job offer, you may believe that it's now smooth sailing. And while getting a job offer is exciting and relieves stress for most candidates, there are a variety of issues that should be considered before you accept any offer. If you only have a single offer that is a good fit for you, you may accept it regardless and thus some of the issues presented below may not seem applicable. Certain issues are germane for people who are considering multiple offers. However, whether you have one or five job offers, the issues provided in this section should be considered so that your final decision is an informed one. This section focuses on how to successfully negotiate an academic package.

The Negotiating Process

Just because you are offered a position does not mean that you are guaranteed the best employment package. You must negotiate for certain resources to be included. Certain items may be nonnegotiable due to institutional or departmental constraints. It is your responsibility to request those resources that will be needed to perform at your best in your new position. Most institutions will provide certain basics (i.e., office space, a computer, conference travel funds, and medical benefits) and determine other resources and perks based on the negotiating process with the candidate. It is important to get as much information as possible to make sure you get the best employment package. Here are eight issues to consider once a job offer has been made.

1. *Celebrate the accomplishment.* Most academic searches are highly competitive. If you have been able to locate a position (especially one that is of most interest to you), this is cause for celebration. Take some time to relish in the occasion—then prepare to begin the negotiating process.

2. *Identify key players and components of the process.* Identify the negotiator. During the interview process, the main contact may have been the chairperson of the search committee. However, a dean, associate dean, or department chairperson may spearhead negotiations. Be sure to determine the appropriate person and direct all questions, comments, and concerns to her or him. Determine what is negotiable and what is not. In many cases, everything is negotiable. Find out whether the process is to initially provide you a contract and then proceed to negotiate. Be sure to stress that your intentions are to make an informed decision based on as much information as possible and to make sure that you are provided with the needed resources to establish a strong research and teaching agenda at the institution. Expect the dean or department chairperson/head to provide most of this information. Items that are typically negotiable include: salary, summer money, teaching load, reduced load for new faculty, the value of your existing publications, committee work, conference fees and travel funding, and relocation expenses. If possible, determine whether the starting salary can vary based on teaching experience and/or publications. Check the Internet for income ranges for positions in your area. These data are important when negotiating salary. Be forthright with questions, but also be careful not to appear greedy, insensitive, and more concerned about financial issues than with the position. Also pose the following types of questions: Are there summer funding opportunities (for example, via grant requests or teaching opportunities, and can one teach and receive a grant during the same period)? What resources will be available (computer, printer in office, software, and voice-mail)? Are relocation funds provided and, if so, what is the amount? What type of travel funding is available (national, regional, statewide)? Are there research leaves and, if so, when? What are the healthcare benefits (vision, life insurance, medical/HMO, dental)? What are the retirement benefits? Can a 401K from a previous position be rolled over? (These latter questions may be referred to the Human Resources

staff.) Be sure to get final decisions in writing before accepting any offer.

3. *List negotiation issues.* Develop a list of questions and/or issues to be negotiated and provide specific justification for each item (being able to justify a higher salary, special resources, or additional travel funds is crucial). The list can be e-mailed or faxed to the appropriate person and items can be reviewed during a conference call or telephone conversation. This approach makes it easier for the institution's negotiator to identify issues that have been addressed and those that require additional feedback before a decision is made. A concise list also suggests that you are professional, thorough, and prepared. Once the negotiator is aware of the items that are open for negotiation, the provost, dean, or department chairperson/head may immediately agree to certain items. Counteroffers may be made to other items. For example, you may request ten computer software packages and the department may agree to purchase six of the ten. You must then determine whether this compromise is acceptable or whether further negotiations regarding computer products are needed. If the items are crucial for performing the job requirements, it would be prudent to request that all ten packages be purchased and provide specific reasons to justify the purchase. Again, justifying the need for certain resources increases the chance they will be provided. Expect delays during this period. Some issues can be addressed quickly; however, the negotiator will typically have to get back to you concerning others. Larger institutions tend to have a more extensive chain of command and thus must contend with more bureaucratic red tape. Some candidates, especially those with a single job offer, may be reluctant to request certain resources. Do not hesitate to ask for those resources that will be needed to fulfill your responsibilities as a new hire. Just as the department will expect you to perform certain tasks, expect the department to provide the necessary resources. If you are unsure about what to request (beyond the resources suggested earlier in this section), also ask new hires in your current department what they consider appropriate resources. However, be mindful that you may require resources unique to your area of focus or discipline (e.g., a research lab, a computer package that is new on the market, or special reference

books and manuals). Ask for those things needed to do your job. Worst case, the department will refuse the request. Best case, they will accept it.

4. *Understand the broader decisionmaking process.* Some institutions require a commitment from the desired candidate in as little as one week while others may extend the consideration time over a slightly longer period. In very competitive markets, some institutions use short decision periods as a strategy to ensure that the position is filled by one of their top candidates. For example, if you are the top candidate and you decide not to accept their offer, they may still have time to contact their next choice before that person is no longer on the market. Despite such potential pressures, be sure to make an informed decision. Do not be pressured into accepting an offer based on limited information. However, it is unprofessional to purposely stall an institution if you can make an employment decision. Get as much information as needed in order to make the best choice. This is especially important if you have several job offers. Remember, an employment decision will directly affect you and your family, so don't be reluctant to ask questions until satisfactory responses are provided to make a comfortable decision. In most cases, after negotiations have been completed and a contract has been signed, it is too late to make major revisions. Thus be careful about feeling compelled to automatically accept a position—even if it is your only offer. Be sure that you are satisfied with the proposed position and the employment package. Give yourself sufficient time to mull over the offer relative to other options, as well as relative to refusing the offer. Gauge the position relative to other positions, potential future interviews at other institutions of interest, nonacademic positions, and other nontraditional academic posts. Seriously and objectively consider the variety of options available. If you don't have other offers, do you expect any? Additional interviews? It may be necessary to contact institutions where you have already interviewed to get a status update about your standing in the selection process. If necessary, ask for an extension. If you feel that a week or several weeks is insufficient time to make a decision (I consider one week insufficient), request that more time is allotted. In some cases, an institution may provide additional time, espe-

cially if there are extenuating circumstances (such as another interview that has already been scheduled and paid for). The institution may not agree, but it does not hurt to ask.

If you are fortunate enough to have multiple offers, inform the current institution of other offers. There is no need to provide specific details about the names of the other colleges and universities, but you will need to inform them about the terms of the other offer(s). Also, notifying the contact person about other interested parties shows forthrightness. Some candidates may use this as a negotiating tactic as well—do this at your own risk, you do not want to appear manipulative. Because of the importance of this subject, I examine it in detail later in this chapter. If you decide to accept a position, notify other institutions that may be seriously considering you. Of equal importance, notify institutions with which you are scheduled to interview in the future. If time permits and you are unsure about the current offer, or interested in another position, you may elect to attend interviews that have already been scheduled. If not, you may always wonder "what if" or have second thoughts about the current position. And an even better position may become available as a result. You should seriously weigh these options. Making other institutions aware that you are no longer on the job market shows professionalism and honesty on your part. If, after careful consideration, you elect to decline an offer, don't feel bad about the decision. While it may be disappointing to the search committee and the interested department, it is most important for you to do what is best for you and your career. Once a decision has been made, do not second guess yourself, move on.

Be sure to confirm the appropriate acceptance method. Most institutions will initially accept an oral agreement over the telephone and require a written statement within a week or a certain number of business days. After negotiations have been completed, the institution will mail you a contract to sign and return to them. If duplicates are not provided, be sure to make a copy of the contract before returning it to the institution. Note your decision on the application schedule (refer to Chapter 4). This is especially important if you decide not to accept a position. In order to be thorough and maintain accurate documentation of the employment search process, it is important to record the status of each position applied for.

5. *Understand departmental constraints.* If a job offer has been extended, the institution is extremely interested in your joining their department. This means that, if possible, they would probably provide most reasonable resource requests. However, every department or program must work within a budget and other institutional constraints. For example, some public institutions are only able to offer certain salaries, no matter how much they would like to offer more. To compensate, they may provide other perks and resources. Be mindful of departmental and institutional constraints so that you can temper your negotiations with tact. It is logical to want to negotiate the best deal and just as institutions attempt to maximize their options so should you. However, serious, direct negotiations do not mean tense negotiations. For example, if you initiate a negative negotiating environment and subsequently accept the position, you may be entering a hostile work environment. In contrast, if an institution seems unwilling to provide basic resources needed (and expected) to perform in the position (e.g., a computer, office space, a competitive salary) and appears hostile regarding inquiries, this may be a sign of a negative work environment.

6. *Solicit advice.* Talk with your graduate program director, dissertation committee chairperson, or academic mentors. Such people may be able to offer advice and negotiating strategies and tactics, appropriate questions, and issues that are specific to your discipline or area. Also, if your graduate department has recently held a job search, contact the search committee chairperson, who will be able to give the perspective of people on the other side of the negotiating table. Their input may be critical. For example, they can provide insight on how to take part in positive negotiations or how to increase the chances of getting certain funds and/or resources. Most importantly, they may be able to inform you about how to best maneuver through the negotiation process without alienating your potential colleagues while garnering those items needed to perform your responsibilities in the new position.

7. *Consider direct and indirect employment benefits.* You may be tempted to focus on the salary associated with a position and overlook other important economic and noneconomic benefits. For example, Position A may pay a little less than the current industry standard, but may offer an outstanding benefits package,

relocation funds, computer resources, travel support, and subsidized faculty housing, and be located in an area with a lower cost of living. In contrast, Position B may provide an excellent salary, but limited medical and retirement benefits and be located in an area with an extremely high cost of living. When the total employment package and other factors are considered, Position A may actually be the better offer. Be sure to consider these types of issues before making a decision. Don't fall into the trap of focusing solely on economic factors or dynamics such as institutional or departmental status.

8. *Don't forget the obvious—finish the dissertation.* I mention this point again for emphasis. For students who are ABD, some positions are contingent upon successful completion of the graduate program (i.e., "Ph.D. in hand"). This means that the position level, title, and salary for the proposed position may change if you do not complete graduate school before starting the job (or a reasonable period thereafter, usually one semester). Some institutions will not allow you to begin a position without the Ph.D. Others may allow you to start, but with a different title (e.g., visiting lecturer rather than assistant professor), status (nontenure-track as opposed to tenure-track), and salary (substantially less than a tenure-track assistant professor). In such cases, candidates are often given a specific, extended period to complete the dissertation or they can be dismissed (even though most departments will attempt to work with you based on the specific circumstances). To forgo these types of challenges, if you are ABD, be sure to complete all graduate school requirements before you begin the new position.

Negotiating Multiple Offers

You've had an extremely successful job search and are now considering multiple job offers. What are some of the issues to be considered? First, it is important to be sure you have written documentation of each offer—especially before you begin to make decisions. Either the dean of the institution or the department head/chairperson is usually responsible for providing the contract. Consider the professional and personal benefits of each offer and rank them. Avoid ranking offers solely based on the salary. Consider the entire package and intangibles such as location and issues relative to your partner, spouse, or children as well. Without providing details, let each institution know that you have multiple offers and that you are considering each one carefully. If a certain offer would be more competitive with certain revisions, let the contact person know. For example, if you are most interested in College A, but the salary is $10,000 less than the offer at College B, inform College A of your concerns (no need to identify the name of College B) so that College A can make a counteroffer if it wishes. Similarly, if you are concerned about the teaching load at College A and have been guaranteed a reduced teaching load for the first two years at College B, request a reduced teaching load at College A. Let College A know whether this issue would be the determining factor for you.

If you have multiple offers, but are still waiting for an update from another institution that is of interest to you, be honest. Inform the other institutions that you are still making a decision and request additional time to do so. Let your contact person at each of the institutions know that your intention is not to "lead them on," but rather to make an informed decision. Request updates from the institution on which you are waiting and impress upon them your need to make a decision. Be mindful that a number of people (faculty, the dean, and business office administrators) are involved in completing contracts and finalizing packages for new hires. It is important to get feedback without becoming overbearing. Be sure to have all your questions answered before making the final decision. If revisions are made to the original contract (for example, you are given a reduced teaching load for the first two years or summer salary for the first three years), be sure to get them in writing either in the contract or as written addendums to the contract. Remember, verbal agreements are not guaranteed to be binding. Be sure to keep your contact people in the information loop as you contemplate which position you will accept.

You want each institution to know that you are seriously considering their offer. Having multiple offers is a great position to be in. However, it can be tenuous. You should be comfortable negotiating for critical resources needed to succeed in your new position and also be willing to compromise regarding issues that would be nice, but aren't as important. Furthermore, although it is important to negotiate (and expected), it should be done in a manner that does not suggest that you are being greedy or potentially using an offer from one institution in order to get a better offer from another institution. Remain positive throughout the process. Be timely and expect timeliness on the part of the institutions. Be sure to remind your contact person that you want the negotiating process to be "win/win" for all involved—as noted earlier, you don't want to appear inflexible and enter with a dark cloud over your reputation because of a poorly executed negotiating process.

■ Handling Employment Rejections

Unfortunately, every academic interview will not result in a job offer. If you have made an onsite visit, the search committee contact will usually inform you if another candidate has been selected for the position. Some candidates learn of a department's decision by contacting them for an update on their employment status. Other candidates who are not selected earlier in the process are usually notified by mail. While it is disappointing to learn that a job offer will not be extended, take the opportunity to update your employment search schedule, improve your job talk, and renew yourself mentally in preparation for the next interview. Without dwelling on an employment rejection, it is important to learn as much as possible to improve your interviewing skills and prepare for subsequent interviews. The following suggestions may be helpful in making the best of an employment rejection.

• *Thank the department.* Although you were not selected for the position, it is still appropriate to send a letter or e-mail to the chairperson of the search committee to thank the department for their consideration. This gesture is a sign of professionalism on your part. It is also appropriate to end interactions positively so that you will be remembered favorably if other positions become available in the future. In addition, faculty interinstitutional networks exist; a good impression at one institution may be conveyed to people at another.

• *Don't panic.* One rejection does not mean that other interviews are not forthcoming or that other job offers will not be made. Remember that you have a variety of other options (refer to Chapter 7). It is important to continue to apply to and interview at other institutions. You may be tempted to wallow in self-pity and second guess your abilities and skills. This is a waste of time and energy. Learn from the experience and immediately anticipate the next interview. Don't take the rejection personally. It is easy to consider a failed job attempt a personal affront. Remember that the decision was a professional one based on professional criteria. Remember the application dynamics. It is easier to put a rejection in the proper perspective if you reflect upon the nature of the application process. Typically a large pool of candidates is vying for a single position. The process is competitive and sometimes another candidate is selected. Given the competitive nature of academia, celebrate your selection to the short list and ability to compete with a small group of stellar candidates. Although you were not selected for the position, reaching that point in the selection process suggests that you may be a serious contender for other positions.

• *Expand your search net.* It may be necessary to reevaluate your application process. This may mean applying to additional institutions, considering postdoctoral, visiting positions, or nonacademic posts, and revising certain application documents. Applying to more positions increases the possibility for future interviews. For some candidates, a nonacademic position may provide economic security until a tenure-track position can be found. For others, such positions may result in exciting career opportunities that had not been considered. Record the decision on your application schedule. Accurately maintaining the status of job offers as well as rejections will complete the application process for each prospective position and help maintain an organized search. Check the timing and reevaluate other positions. Do you expect to hear from other institutions soon? How many responses are outstanding? If several weeks have passed and you have not received a status update concerning other positions you have applied for, contact the search committee chairperson to learn your status. Determine outstanding applications for which you do not have an interview, rejection letter, or request for additional information. For example, if you recently applied to several institutions and the application deadline is a month in the future, you will not be contacted until after the deadline, while you can expect to hear from institutions you applied to several months ago much sooner. In the latter situation, it is also appropriate to contact them for a status update. Also, if you have heard from all other institutions you have applied to, it would be prudent to apply to additional institutions and/or consider other employment options. If, on the other hand, you have not been notified by some institutions, contact them to determine if you are being seriously considered for an interview or if an offer will be made (note: some academics suggest that your graduate adviser should make such queries).

• *Meet with your mentor.* Have a meeting with your mentor or people who have advised you during the application process to evaluate your status and brainstorm about future tactics. It is important to get opinions from people who may have a different perspective on the subject. You may have difficulty assessing your status objectively because you are too close to the process. Objective third parties are important.

• *Consider remaining in your graduate department.* If you do not foresee other interviews and offers, it will be necessary to determine other options. Should you continue to search next year? Should you consider institutions that you had ignored during earlier phases of the search? It may be necessary to locate employment elsewhere while you continue the academic search. Your current department may offer visiting lecturer or instructor positions. Getting such a post would enable you to continue the job search for another year, remain connected to academia, strengthen your teaching skills, get a grant, or possibly improve your publication record. Another added benefit—by remaining at your graduate school, you would have access to familiar faculty, resources, and environment.

7

Other Employment Options

The objective of most people reading this book is to locate a tenure-track academic position in a specific discipline. This chapter presents information about less-noted academic positions as well as nonacademic opportunities. For some graduate students, joint appointments will represent viable academic options that they might not have otherwise considered. And sobering statistics and reality means that there are a finite number of tenure-track academic positions available yearly. Thus some qualified candidates will have unsuccessful traditional searches and will have to consider nontenure-track positions. Postdoctoral positions and nontraditional academic and nonacademic positions represent potential opportunities for involvement directly and/or indirectly in academic endeavors, to develop research and teaching skills and credentials, and to establish networks necessary for subsequent academic employment searches.

■ Joint Appointments

A joint position is a tenure-track post in which you are responsible to two departments or a department and a program at a given institution. These types of positions will require you to have distinct roles and responsibilities in two areas. For example, a joint position may be available in political science and American studies where a faculty member teaches, performs research, and has service roles in each area. Although there are numerous benefits to joint positions, many graduating students do not consider them.

Joint positions can provide you with an opportunity to expand your pool of employment options. Many candidates may not consider these types of positions because they are unaware that they exist or aren't sure they have the credentials to successfully apply. While these types of posts are available less frequently, there are a variety of benefits that should be considered. First, joint positions offer you the ability to expand your research interests beyond the typical structure. Remember, joint appointees are *expected* to have cross- and multidisciplinary interests and are encouraged to pursue those interests that will benefit each department or program. Such expectations can also encourage a more varied research agenda. In addition, involvement in several areas provides additional opportunities to establish networks, professional alliances, and research collaboration with a wider array of faculty.

Although the benefits of joint appointments are numerous, be mindful of several challenges. Contrary to what may be unconsciously expected at some institutions, a joint position does not mean two positions. And although you should not be expected to have double duty, people with these types of positions may experience unrealistic expectations on the part of faculty from the two departments/programs. This point cannot be emphasized enough. To minimize these types of problems, before you accept a joint appointment, request a list of clear, specific departmental/program responsibilities and expectations from each area in writing. (Note: If you accept a joint position, notify department chairpersons/ heads if you later feel the joint status is unduly taxing.) However, candidates who seek such positions must be able to balance the responsibilities associated with dual accountability. This means managing time wisely, maintaining a strong level of communication with each area head or director, and coordinating roles and tasks between the two. The following important formal and informal issues should be addressed in writing.

Formal Issues
• *Department time.* Does the position require 50 percent of your time in each department or program? Sixty percent in one department and 40 percent in another? Seventy/thirty? Keep in mind that departmental divisions other than 50/50 may be difficult to measure and follow.

• *Course load.* How many courses will you teach in each area? For example, a typical 50/50 division at an institution with a teaching load of two courses per semester would require you to teach one course in each department/program each semester.

• *Committee work.* What are the committee responsibilities? Will you be expected to serve on more committees in a certain department/program than in another? How will this be determined and by whom?

• *Tenure process.* How are tenure considerations made for joint appointees? Does the process differ when compared to traditional appointees? If so, why and how? Is one department/program the tenure-granting department while the other only provides a letter of reference? What is the past tenure granting record for joint appointees at the institution and in the specific department/program? If you are considering a joint position, get a clear understanding of how tenure is decided for joint appointees *before* you accept the post.

• *Office space.* Will separate offices or office space be provided in each department/program? Will you have to share space with other faculty members?

• *Resources.* What resources (such as computers, printer, telephone, and copying privileges) will each department/program provide? What steps must be completed to obtain resources?

• *New or existing process.* Has the department or program hired joint appointees before? How have they worked out? Are there other joint appointees in the same position or areas in which you are applying? Can you contact them for additional information about the position? For some institutions, joint appointments are quite commonplace and the process is a smooth one because departments/programs have a well-established routine for such positions. Institutions that are just establishing joint appointments may experience a learning curve that can result in problems for candidates who accept them.

In general, it is best to clearly outline requirements and responsibilities in both departments/programs. A variety of less formal, but important, considerations should also be made. Answers to these types of questions, unfortunately, are often more difficult to ascertain and may require you to read between the lines or seek candid advice from current joint appointees or other faculty members. However, answers to such queries can be the difference between a positive experience and a problematic one.

Informal Issues

• *Interdisciplinary support and respect.* What is the relationship between the two departments/programs? Do they view each other favorably? Will your research and teaching be considered credible and valuable by both? For example, if you perform qualitative research that is valued by a program but is valued less by the tenure-granting department, this will probably pose problems should you accept the position.

• *Complementary vs. competing interests.* Can the work done on behalf of one department/program enhance the other? Do the departments/programs have competing or divergent methodologies or theoretical foci? Do faculty from each unit understand how you will fit into their area and recognize the value of your potential contributions?

• *Relationship between department chairpersons/heads or program directors.* Do the department chairpersons/heads or program directors get along with each other? Do they work well together? Have they established joint arrangements in the past and did the process run smoothly?

• *Administrative receptivity.* In general, how receptive is the institution to joint positions? Do departments/programs get support for these types of posts or does the institution frown on arrangements other than traditional tenure-track positions?

• *Institution type.* Is the joint appointment offered by a research institution or teaching college? How established is its joint program? In some cases, larger institutions may have a more established joint process, which means that a candidate that accepts a position knows that it is a structured, organized program that has worked well in the past.

If you plan to apply for a joint appointment, assess the position based on your personal objectives and be sure to speak with other people who hold similar positions. In addition, prepare in graduate school by taking the necessary courses to make you well rounded as a teacher and researcher in several areas. It is unwise to believe that membership in a particular group is a necessary or sufficient condition for selection for a joint appointment. For example, just because you are a psychology major of Hispanic decent does not automatically make you an appropriate candidate for a joint position in the psychology and Latino studies departments (even if the prospective institution thinks you are). Determine whether your course background and research experience and interests will contribute to both areas. There may, in fact, be a white male or an Asian female candidate who is a better fit for that joint position. Last, assess your time-management skills to be sure you are able to organize and structure responsibilities to effectively and efficiently meet the requirements and demands of both appointments.

▓ Visiting Positions, Postdoctoral Programs and Fellowships, and Nonacademic Posts

Although this book focuses on locating a traditional position in academia, you should be aware of other employment opportunities, some of which are outside of academia. Many such positions allow you to use your research and teaching skills in ways that are similar to academia. In addition, many nonacademic institutions also inform the academy (e.g., the Centers for Disease Control in Atlanta, GA). In addition, some positions are more financially lucrative and may allow for an easier transition back into academia if you desire to re-enter your chosen field. When evaluating nontraditional academic positions and nonacademic posts, consider the following types of questions:

- Why am I considering the position? If I had an academic offer, would I still consider this position?
- Can the position allow me to use the skills developed in graduate school? Will the position require some of the same types of activities (e.g., presenting at conferences, lecturing or presenting during meetings)? Am I comfortable with the differences? Does the position offer opportunities for intellectual challenge and growth and interaction with an intellectual com-

munity of scholars or peers? Will the position allow for publishing opportunities if I desire them?

- Will it be difficult to move back into a traditional academic position if I want to do so? What are the drawbacks of taking such a position if I want to return to academia later?
- Are there benefits associated with the position that are not available in an academic post?
- What do my mentors, faculty members, and dissertation committee members think about the position? What advice do they give? What do my family and friends think about the position?

Visiting Positions

Visiting positions are typically one- to two-year contractual positions that reflect many of the responsibilities of a tenure-track post. A visiting professor may be required to teach several courses and has access to institutional resources such as a computer and office space to perform research. Visiting instructors or visiting lecturers may be required to teach more courses than visiting professors and may not have some of the perks. Instructors and lecturers are often paid based on the number of courses they teach. In general, benefits such as salary and insurance will vary by institution. Whether a position is presented as a professor, instructor, or lecturer may be a matter of semantics at some institutions. However, the name of the post usually reflects the focus, scope, resources, and benefits it provides. Such positions are usually offered to fill short-term teaching needs and do not include any guarantee that they will continue after the specified period. However, if you were unable to locate a tenure-track post, a visiting position may be a viable option to consider—especially if you plan to remain in academia for a subsequent search the following year.

There are potential benefits as well as drawbacks associated with visiting posts. A visiting position enables people to work in academia and have many responsibilities commensurate with a tenure-track post. In addition, you would still have access to other academics for networking purposes as a member of an academic community. And although it would not be a tenure-track position, such a post, when included on the vita, would be considered more akin to a traditional academic position than employment further removed from teaching and/or research. Although the salaries tend to be lower than those of tenure-track positions, such positions address general concerns about unemployment. I have also known of people who began their careers at an institution in a visiting post that later became a tenure-track position. In other instances, the department may perform a search for which the visiting faculty member would be encouraged to apply. In the latter case, a visiting professor/instructor/lecturer who has performed well may have a slight advantage over other potential candidates because he/she has already shown evidence of the ability to be successful in that department. However, in other instances, an institution is only interested in hiring a person for a finite period. Thus if you are considering a visiting post, ask the contact person about the likelihood of the position becoming tenure-track. Best case, you may be able to transition into a tenure-track position; worst case, you have academic employment for a specific period.

There are several limitations to note regarding visiting posts. Usually because of the teaching load (three to four courses per semester), it is difficult to establish and maintain a research agenda. This issue will not be a concern for candidates interested in tenure-track posts at teaching institutions, but may be a problem for those whose ultimate objective is to locate a traditional post at a research institution. Some positions may require you to teach four related, but different, courses, which means four separate "preps" and the corresponding outlay of time and energy. Last, some visiting positions are only for a one-year period. In such a situation, you will have to determine whether it is worth it to relocate yourself (and possibly your family) for such a short period of time. When considering a visiting position, weigh the pros and cons of the post to determine whether and how it will help you meet your ultimate objective of locating a tenure-track position (ask about a possible visiting position at your current institution, for reasons discussed in the section titled Handling Employment Rejections in Chapter 6).

Postdoctoral Programs and Fellowships

A postdoctoral position (often referred to as a postdoc) or a fellowship can provide you with the financial support and resources to perform advanced research in your field for an extended period of time. These types of options can offer certain benefits over a traditional position in academia. They can be excellent opportunities for people who wish to focus on research rather than teaching before searching for a tenure-track position. In addition, some postdocs provide opportunities to work in academia for people who are unable to locate a traditional position or who are not interested in a traditional academic career at this time. In some cases, people have the opportunity to be mentored by top scholars in their field and also to work with other rising peers.

A fellowship or postdoctoral position at a prestigious university or in a well-known department or program can be used to bolster your publishing record, establish professional networks, strengthen presentation skills, and possibly catapult your career. In some cases, a postdoctoral stint or fellowship can provide you with the publishing record and contacts to be more competitive in the traditional academic market if and when you re-enter it later. Some graduate students have chosen this option rather than accept a traditional position they believe to be less than ideal or one that may divert them from certain career aspirations. And in some disciplines, graduate students are expected to work for two to three years at a postdoc before entering the traditional academic market. Institutions such as Cornell University, University of Michigan, and Harvard University often provide such opportunities. Some positions are quite competitive, but can prove to be invaluable for selected candidates.

If you are considering postdoctoral and other fellowship positions, be mindful of a few issues. It will be important to maintain contact with faculty members from your graduate program for letters of reference if you wish to re-enter the job market for a tenure-track position. Also, monitor the time spent outside traditional academia. If extremely long periods elapse, it may be more difficult to re-enter the market and locate a tenure-track post. Some institutions may be suspicious of candidates who have held a variety of postdocs over long periods of time, but have never held a tenure-track position, because they question why such a person has not located a tenure-track job. Candidates with extensive postdoc experience should be able to justify their positions and explain their chosen career trajectory as well as their return to traditional academia.

Nonacademic Posts

These types of organizations employ a variety of people from academia (social scientists, engineers, social workers, political scientists, mathematicians, researchers, and scientists). Some positions only require a master's degree, but many require Ph.D.s and provide opportunities for research and teaching similar to that found in academia. In addition, some positions can provide significantly higher salaries than those in academia and include perks such as travel, the opportunity to manage a staff, autonomy, and greater upward mobility. You may find exciting, rewarding careers in the following types of arenas. Note that, in many instances, examples are provided of specific companies, institutions, and positions.

- Nonprofit research organizations (e.g., Baldwin & Associates)
- Online textbook publishers, multidisciplinary and within your discipline, such as Digital Learning Interactive, Digital Textbook Developer, and Wizeup Digital Textbooks, provide texts in fields such as accounting, business, economics, English, finance, philosophy, psychology, and sociology. Furthermore, university and commercial academic presses may have positions for people with advanced degrees
- For-profit research firms may offer research associate positions
- Nonprofit organizations on college campuses; for example, the Los Angeles Caregiver Resource Center located on the campus of the University of Southern California provides a variety of family services for families of brain-impaired people and employs a variety of professionals such as site supervisors, family consultants, and intake specialists
- Research centers associated with a university or college may offer positions such as project directors or grant writers
- Technological, computer, and research and development firms offer positions such as project directors or project managers that often require a Ph.D.
- The Centers for Disease Control employs project managers
- The Census Bureau offers a variety of technical and management positions that often cross disciplines

- Independent consultants, for example, are employed as program evaluators, statistical consultants for engineering firms, linguists, or political scientists
- The Population Council employs research associates in a variety of divisions
- RAND Corporation has positions for demographers, sociologists, and statisticians
- Social policy organizations employ administrators and research associates with a quantitative and/or qualitative research background
- Marketing firms, such as Strategic Marketing Corporation in Bala Cynwyd, PA, employ academics who specialize in pharmaceutical/healthcare marketing research in project management positions. In these positions, people are required to perform research and publish findings
- Online universities, such as Vcampus
- Academic web sites, such as Mascotnetwork
- Community colleges or local technical schools
- Human resources departments
- Grassroots organizations that employ political advisers and managers
- Think tanks

Grants and Fellowships to Consider

- Foundations, for example, the Ford Foundation, offer positions such as grant and program directors
- Rockefeller Foundation in Humanities *www.rockfound.org*
- National Science Foundation *www.nsf.gov*
- National Endowment for the Humanities *www.neh.gov*
- Nonprofit Sector Research Fund *nsrf@aspeninstitute.org*
- The Japan Foundation Center for Global Partnership *info@cgp.org*
- Fullbright Scholar *www.cies.org*
- Harry Ransom Humanities Research Center *www.lib.utexas.edu/hrc/*

- Boston University visiting research fellowships
  www.bu.edu/irsd/
- The Rutgers Center for Historical Analysis
  http://rcha.rutgers.edu
- Radcliffe Institute Fellowships *www.radcliffe.edu*
- Mellon postdoctoral fellowships in the humanities
  www.arts.cornell.edu/sochum/

The general online source for information on fellowships and research opportunities is *www.orau.gov/orisc/educ.htm.*

Other Teaching Opportunities to Consider

- High schools
- Preparatory schools
- Community colleges/two-year institutions

■ General Nonemployment Considerations

You were determined to locate a tenure-track position and the position you selected did not meet your expectations. Or you concertedly searched for a tenure-track post and did not locate one. In each scenario, a certain degree of disappointment is expected. People in the former situation are challenged to identify benefits in their new position (such as teaching and mentoring students, performing research and expanding current literature) and consider the implications of re-entering the market the following year. People in the latter scenario are challenged to objectively assess their options for employment, remain undaunted, and prepare for future search opportunities. Remember that employment competition can vary by year and that it is common for initial searches to be less than ideal. Also realize that changes can be made. Although certain academic moves may be more difficult than others (e.g., locating a position at a research institution after a long period at a teaching institution or returning to academia after a long career in a nonacademic post), many choices are dynamic and there is a certain degree of fluidity even in these types of deci-

sions. If, for example, you choose one position and come to realize it is not best for you, you can always re-enter the market in the
future. Or if you do not locate a tenure-track position, this does
not mean that other opportunities aren't available and that a
tenure-track post cannot be located during a subsequent search.
You always have the option to change and make changes (refer to
Chapter 10 about re-entering the job market), but it is important to
be informed about possibilities, constraints, and consequences of
your decisions.

8

A Personal Fit

You've received an invitation for an interview. You excitedly begin to plan. This means deciding the scope of your academic presentation, how to organize the teaching presentation, what you will wear, and the types of questions you will ask department members. Many times, candidates focus so much attention on the professional dimensions of the onsite interview and the professional issues when they are deciding whether or not to accept a position that they neglect to address personal matters that can influence their professional careers and quality of life. Just as overlooking important professional issues during the academic job search can have dramatic repercussions, so can overlooking personal ones. Remember that no matter how great the employment package, if the position is not a personal fit, it can undermine your ability to succeed on the job. Although you will spend a great deal of time inside the walls of academia—teaching in the classroom and performing research—you will also spend a great deal of time *outside of academia.* Thus it is important to consider personal issues as well as professional ones.

Some candidates may feel unable to evaluate a position in terms of personal issues. For example, if you have been on the market for an entire year and have a single job offer, you may feel pressured by advisers, other faculty, peers, and family to accept the offer even if you have personal concerns (e.g., about the location of the institution). On the other hand, if you have several offers, you may feel more comfortable weighing personal as well as professional concerns. This is not the appropriate approach to take. Even if you only have one job offer, you should still investigate the institution relative to your expected quality of life. If you decide that your personal concerns outweigh your desire to accept the position, you may decide to remain on the job market or expand your options and consider nontraditional employment. Regardless of your decision, the important thing to remember is— you must consider quality of life issues.

This chapter focuses on personal issues that should be assessed as you search for a position and decide whether or not to accept a certain post. My basic contention is that you should search for a position that meets your professional *and* personal needs. Each of these elements is essential. Although this topic is being discussed late in the book, it is by no means an unimportant factor. In fact, some would suggest that personal issues are the most important factors to consider. For example, Candidate A may accept a position in which he earns less money and teaches more courses, but where the quality of life is ideal for him. Candidate B may accept a position in which he earns $10,000 more than the median salary in his discipline, but he feels isolated in his department and in the community. If we examine both scenarios, many people would conclude that Candidate A got "the best deal" because he has a better quality of life.

■ The Importance of Quality of Life

What exactly is quality of life and why is it important? Of course the term means different things to different people. The goal here is not to provide a precise definition, but rather to broadly define the concept, identify some of its important components, and understand its importance relative to selecting an academic position. In this context, quality of life refers to the characteristics, properties, or features of your personal experiences as an academic. Quality of life refers to the kind of private life and the nature of your social life *outside* of academia. Quality of life reflects one's lifestyle. For some it reflects work-family balance, parental leave policies, proximity to extended family, or availability of employment for one's partner or spouse. For others it includes a sense of being settled, issues of safety, acceptance in a community, or feeling comfortable in an area. It can also include availability and access to social events and the friendliness and receptivity of people in a city, town, community, department, or program. You must decide what quality of life means to you. Do you need a local church that is similar in ideology to your current congregation? Do you need social events geared toward single people? Are well-established elementary and middle schools with good track records central to you? Or are you interested in living in a city with a large ethnic community? What are your *basic requirements* for happiness and well-being outside academia?

Of course, quality of life issues are highly subjective and require more work to determine than some issues related to the professional side of the academic search. In order to effectively assess quality of life issues, you will need to identify and prioritize your personal needs. Doing so will require you to project and predict, to think about the type of life you wish to lead based on your personal needs. For example, if your research and publishing in your new position are going well, your teaching and student mentoring are rewarding, and you get great evaluations, but you spend most weekends alone or with little to do, will this be sufficient for you? It is important to remember that the personal can overshadow the professional. A poor, stagnant, or nonexistent personal life can undermine the best academic position and accomplishments. Simply put, you don't want to love your job and hate your life. These two dimensions should complement and enhance each other. Also, be careful not to equate quality of life with an employment package. Yes, they affect each other (it will be hard to maintain a social life if you are not paid adequately), but they are not the same. Given the significance of one's personal life, it is startling that many candidates weigh academic options without considering personal issues.

You can help ensure that your personal needs are met by considering them just as you do professional issues. This means determining and weighing personal needs as well as professional ones, viewing employment packages more holistically, and having a basic set of standards that are meaningful to you. There is no magic balance of professional and personal needs. The best fit for you will be one that realistically takes into consideration your academic career as well as your quality of life. What happens if you don't consider personal issues? Well, some of your personal needs will be met, others might be, and many may not. If you do not proactively consider your personal needs, you increase the odds that they will not be addressed—and you may ultimately face negative experiences that undermine your new academic career.

It is important to realize that no position or place will be perfect. The sooner you accept this truth, the better you can realistically and objectively evaluate potential positions based on both professional and personal criteria. Expect to compromise. Decide early what factors are essential for your quality of life and which ones would be nice, but aren't necessary. And although personal needs will vary from one candidate to the next, there are some common expectations to consider. This next section addresses topics of academic and nonacademic climate, family, and general personal issues.

■ The Academic Climate

The importance of this topic cannot be emphasized enough. During your campus visit, be sure to assess the overall academic climate as well as the climate in the prospective department/program. Has the campus been the site of student unrest? Are colleagues and/or students known to show hostility toward female professors or professors of color? Does the academic community have a less than cordial relationship with the local community (town vs. gown)? Has the department had problems with retention of junior faculty, in-office schisms, or methodological and ideological differences? These types of issues influence the academic climate and can stymie your success. For example, if you are considering a position at a teaching college where your tenure is determined primarily by student evaluations and the courses you will teach are especially rigorous or controversial, these issues can directly impact the classroom environment, course evaluations, and your subsequent bid for tenure. Or does your research methodology differ drastically from that of most members of the department and is it less valued in the discipline? If so, it would be wise to consider the ramifications of accepting such a position. This does not mean that a post should be automatically rejected. However, if possible, have a candid conversation with the department chairperson/head and with other faculty members during your campus visit to assess how your research approach or teaching responsibilities will be received in the department and what this could mean relative to your career there.

Some of these issues may not be important enough to warrant rejecting an offer, but they should be considered because they can influence quality of life at work. It is probably best to ask such questions during one-on-one interview sessions with the department chairperson/head, or during lunch or dinner with a small group of faculty, rather than in a large group setting such as during the job talk presentation. Questions such as, "What would you say have been the most challenging situations the department has faced in the last two years?" or "I'm interested in learning about the inner-workings of the department. Could you tell me about a particularly difficult issue the department had to deal with and how it was addressed?" may help to broach the subject in a non-threatening, professional manner.

I recall a particularly negative campus visit during my academic search. Much to the chagrin of attendees, I was verbally attacked by a faculty member who continually attempted to undermine my job talk presentation. Although apologies were extended and I was subsequently offered a position, no amount of money would compensate for the suggested hostile academic climate that would have probably only compounded upon my arrival as a faculty member. While this experience was an isolated one (most of my job talks were very enjoyable), I present it here to remind you not to overlook experiences, comments, and behavior that may be indicators of less than collegial departmental climates. If you have a negative encounter during your campus visit or have some concerns about the campus or department climate, try to determine whether your concerns are individualistic or systemic—was your experience an isolated one based on a particular person or do you think your experience was indicative of the overall climate (in my example, I believed the problem to be systemic). If you can attribute your concerns to a single person, it may not represent a major concern (you can expect to encounter a few unprofessional people). However, if you believe there is an unhealthy setting in a department or program, it is best to avoid such a position. Others may disagree, but it is a decision only you can make.

Just as an unhealthy academic climate should be avoided, realize the benefits of locating employment in a department/program where members are collegial, supportive of each other's research and ideological and methodological differences, and concerned about the well-being of junior faculty. If the prospective department is small, consider potential interactions with colleagues from other, related departments. You cannot place a dollar value on such an environment. A positive academic climate is especially important for new faculty members. In many instances, even the most qualified, well-prepared junior faculty member will need assistance from faculty members to learn the ropes. This means becoming familiar with the department/program culture, structure, and process, locating mentors and research collaborators, getting help to develop courses, or just having someone to talk with on challenging days (be comfortable considering people outside your immediate department). A positive academic environment may prevent you as a new faculty member from having to reinvent the wheel in terms of teaching and/or implementing your research agenda. Finally, it is important to note that, while an academic arena should be conducive to your career, it is unrealistic to expect all colleagues to be open and receptive. So you should not necessarily be searching for an academic arena that will provide you with a myriad of "best friends" but, rather, one that reflects a collegial, professional environment.

■ The Nonacademic Climate

Much of a new faculty member's time is spent preparing new courses, collecting data, and/or performing research, serving on committees, and mentoring students. However, you will not spend all of your time on campus. For this reason, consider the nonacademic climate of prospective institutions as well. As mentioned before, there should be a reasonable balance between your professional and personal life. During the campus visit, request that time be set aside to briefly tour the local community and get information about social venues, national sites, ethnic enclaves, historic districts, and other places of interest to you. Request that the search committee chairperson arrange an area tour with a real estate agent during your campus visit as another mechanism to gather information about the nonacademic climate.

If you are seriously interested in a position, request to stay in town an additional day to tour the area. With a little early planning, this can be done. Ask for an interview period near the weekend and request a return flight on Sunday night or Monday. This will give you the weekend to tour the area, locate the campus/community listings of social venues and sites, and just mill around. Most institutions will honor such a request because staying the weekend typically results in cheaper airfare. However, unless the area has a good mass transit system, you will need a rental car or a guide (given your interest in the position, it would be money well spent to pay for your own rental car if the department can't). Gathering information about the state and possibly the city/town via the Internet will also help you study the environment around the campus and gather important nonacademic information such as cost of living, housing and rental fees, traffic, available public transportation, quality and number of important service providers, and crime statistics.

If you are offered a position and if the location is not too far from your current home, it may be helpful to visit the community again to get a better feel for it (some departments may pay for or subsidize such a trip). During the weekend, visit local grocery stores, libraries, restaurants, malls, museums, religious institutions, theatres, and other businesses. Note their services, how people interact with you, and the caliber and quantity of products. Determine whether the climate is similar to your current place of residence. If you sense there are major differences, you will have to decide whether they should be key factors in your decisionmaking process.

While you should discuss the nonacademic climate with department members, it is also a good idea to talk with locals. Residents not affiliated with the campus may be able to give you a different portrait of the city, town, or community as compared to academics. They may also be more knowledgeable about the history of the community, any challenges it has faced, and its relationship with the campus community. This means starting a conversation with a waitress during lunch, asking questions of the clerk at a store in the mall or an elderly couple at the library, or speaking with clergy at the local parish. Again, typically this level of involvement cannot take place during your initial campus visit when you will be focused on getting the job, but rather following the initial visit (an extended weekend) or during a subsequent trip.

Finally, the relationship between the academic and nonacademic communities should be noted. As a rule of thumb, more culturally diverse institutions are often located in large cities or urban centers. However, an institution located in a small, rural area can purposely create a diverse campus atmosphere by recruiting a diverse faculty. But because the nonacademic community often "feeds" the academic one in the form of local students, staff, and long-time faculty from the area, expect the two climates to influence one another (I wager this is especially true of institutions located in small towns where many of its employees are local residents).

Partners and Children

If you are married or have a partner, a significant other, or children, you will also need to consider their quality of life in a new locale. Many of the issues raised earlier will apply to them as well. However, there are several other issues specific to mates and children that should be considered. Will the prospective institution assist in locating employment for your significant other? If he/she is in academia, will a spousal hire position be an option? If so, what will be the logistics for such an offer and when should it be expected? Many institutions realize the importance of minimizing the relocation efforts of new hires. This may also mean helping them locate jobs for their mates. Some schools have recruitment offices in place or provide opportunities for qualified mates to interview for staff positions on campus. By providing employment assistance for mates, institutions are helping to ensure that the desired candidate accepts the position and is retained. One of the easiest ways to lose a candidate is to fail to provide relocation assistance for mates (or if the mate cannot locate gainful employment in the future, the new hire's departure may be imminent) or to neglect to be helpful in the transition process for their mates in appropriate ways. Be sure to ask your contact whether spousal hiring is an option or if job placement services are offered. However, only make this request after you have been offered the job because you want the search committee to make decisions about you based on your profile and onsite interview and not relative to this additional potential challenge.

Your excitement about a position can also wane if important basic resources are not available for your children. This means asking questions about the number and quality of public elementary, middle, and high schools, and the availability of private schools. How are the schools ranked in terms of national test scores and other criteria? Graduation rates? Student-teacher ratios? College placement rates? Diversity appreciation? Are they similar to the types of schools your children currently attend or do they differ dramatically? Visiting several schools before accepting a job may be helpful in answering these types of questions. Just as you should consider issues of quality of life for this new phase of your life, it is necessary to do so for your children as such transitions are sometimes more challenging for them. If you have small children, day care may be of central importance. Find out whether day care is available on- or off-campus and whether it is subsidized by the institution. Ask members of the department about the day care facilities they use, waiting lists, costs, and playgroups, and how they balance their jobs and childcare responsibilities (note: some academics disagree with this suggestion because of concerns that a candidate may be negatively stereotyped for seeming overly concerned about domestic issues). Of equal importance is the number and caliber of local hospitals and the distance from more comprehensive facilities. This is especially important if the campus is located in a rural or isolated area. Other interests may include the availability of children's museums and learning centers. The Internet is a good starting point for gathering this type of information, but it would still be prudent to speak with select academics and local residents about resources and support networks for mates and children.

More About Academic Spousal Hiring

Given the commitment involved in earning a Ph.D., many graduate students spend a great deal of time on campus, in classes, and in academic settings. It seems logical that many would meet their life partner there. It is becoming increasingly common for candidates to be married to or in a relationship with someone who is an academic or who will be entering the academic job market. Although I mentioned this issue in an earlier section, there is need to provide more information on the subject because it may bring about a unique set of professional and personal challenges for you, some of which can be proactively addressed, others of which may be out of your hands. Note that I focus on marriage here because many institutions that consider spousal arrangements only recognize legally established unions (however, if the prospective institution recognizes partners, these issues apply).

If you are married to an academic or soon-to-be academic, you must consider her/his future in academia as well. This means evaluating your prospective positions based on whether there are openings for your spouse. For example, if the English department at Scott University is very interested in you, would the biology department consider your spouse for an academic post? Does biology need someone in your mate's particular area of research? Are they currently involved in a search or have they been given permission to initiate one? If a position is possibly available, will it be a tenure-track post, visiting lecturer position, or laboratory research post? How will this be decided? And is your spouse open to being considered for a post in which he or she may only be indirectly interested? Does your spouse have concerns about how the department will receive him or her (i.e., will your spouse be recognized for potential contributions to the area or simply be someone they "had to hire" in order to accommodate another department or program)?

Given that most departments and programs only search for positions that need to be filled, your spouse's credentials may be stellar, but the department may not have a need for another scholar in that area. While some institutions regularly make such arrangements and are on the lookout for "opportunity hires" (stellar candidates who may not fill a pressing departmental need, but who will enhance the overall research and teaching in the unit), others directly or indirectly discourage such hiring practices. Other institutions may be interested in spousal hiring, but have difficulty coordinating the process between the two departments/programs (both must be open to this option). And some departments realize that locating an academic post for your spouse will increase the chances that you will accept their position and also that an academic couple will be retained in the area.

If the prospective department considers spousal hires, you must determine how your spouse feels about the possibility. Remember, just as you are searching for the "ideal position," this is your spouse's goal as well. And while, in this situation, both of you will have to compromise to some degree, be sure that your spouse is open to being considered and that he/she meets the academic requirements for a position. If your mate is a stellar candidate, this may alleviate concerns about not being considered based on merit. It may also alleviate department members' concerns that they are being forced to accept a mediocre new colleague (note that the second department or program should coordinate the logistics for your spouse's campus visit). Finally, it may be the case that your spouse (and not you) is able to locate a position at an institution that will also consider you for a post. In this case, you become the potential spousal hire and must consider the above issues.

■ Personal Strategies and Suggestions to Consider

Just as you should consider a variety of professional issues, consider the following personal issues and strategies before accepting a position.

• *Think about how long you plan to stay in a position.* Given that you are thinking about accepting an offer to start a new position, this suggestion may seem premature. But establishing an estimated career timeline can help place quality of life issues in the proper context. Do you plan to remain at your first institution until tenure (i.e., six years) and then relocate to another place? Do you view the position as a stepping stone and plan to look for other opportunities each year? Or are you looking for a place to live long term or until your children graduate from high school? Each candidate may have a different set of timing issues and projections. But if your plan is short term, you may be less concerned about major quality of life issues. If, however, you plan to remain in a position at least until tenure, quality of life will be an important factor to consider (note: remember that if you decide to leave, you must begin a new job search with no guarantee of success). Also accept that relocating means leaving certain aspects of your current lifestyle behind. Even if you land the ideal position in the ideal place for you, things will still be different. In most cases, you won't have access to current friends and family, old "stomping grounds," or familiar faces and places. So even if most of your quality of life issues are addressed in a new locale, there will still be a period of adjustment.

• *Seek out campuses with diverse departments/programs.* Institutions with educational options such as Jewish Studies, Latino Studies, Queer Studies, African American Studies, Women's Studies, and Asian Studies suggest diversity in action. This shows that an institution has committed a certain amount of resources to multiculturalism and to providing educational opportunities for students to learn about such topics. Such institutions may also be part of a larger, culturally diverse, tolerant, and socially aware community. Also consider institution size and type. Large institutions typically have a variety of on-campus organizations that sponsor weekly programs and events and are able to bring in nationally acclaimed speakers, singing groups, plays, and other productions. Most also have sports teams. Smaller colleges, especially comprehensive liberal arts institutions, usually have a calendar of social events geared toward exposing students and staff to an array of intellectual and cultural events. While their programs may be smaller in scale to those of larger institutions, most are quite diverse in topic and scope. These types of events, often free for students and offered at reduced rates for faculty, staff, and the community, represent outlets that can be both academic and social in nature.

• *Prioritize your personal needs.* Identify your major and minor needs and list them from most to least important. The list should include emotional (network of friends and acquaintances), psychological (feeling of safety in the community), and health-related (proximity to hospitals) issues, to name a few. This will enable you to specify those things that are central to good quality of life and to try to determine whether they are available in the location to which you may move. Note that some of your needs will be more abstract than others (emotional support versus proximity to good schools) and it will be more challenging to determine whether these needs can be met. However, listing and prioritizing them is an important step in proactively working toward having your personal needs met. Distinguish needs from wants. Realistically, no location will meet all your personal requirements, but some will do a better job than others. It's important to determine those needs that have to be met and those that you could live without.

• *Take your family on a familiarization trip.* Once you decide on a position of interest, it may be beneficial to take family members who will also have to relocate to visit the new locale. This will enable your mate to visit places that will be important to him/her and for children to do the same. This should probably be done after an offer has been extended and if you have some questions about the community. Be especially cognizant of potential "town vs. gown" issues. Decide what this concept means in the prospective location and what it may mean to you as a potential resident. In some instances, the local community may have a less than favorable relationship with the academic institution. If this is the case, some thought should be given to what strained relationships may mean to you on a daily basis. This may not be reason enough to decline a position, but it may influence your quality of life. Determine the nature of the community. Is the area very traditional? Racially and/or ethnically homogeneous? Do most outlets focus on married couples with children with few options for single people? Issues of "town vs. gown" may take on new meaning for candidates from underrepresented groups. In addition, don't expect to automatically connect with local residents simply because of racial/ethnic heritage or group similarity. For example, you may be considered a "transplant." Also, don't assume suspicions are based on race/ethnicity; in some cases, class or socioeconomic status may be a factor. Be sure to investigate the cultural climate in the area relative to diversity. No matter the community, realize that it will take time to gain entry.

• *Consider the type of appointment and research objectives.* Certain positions lend themselves to travel outside one's area. Will your research involve traveling abroad to collect data? Collecting archival data at remote regional sites? Quarterly clinical conferences? If so, even positions in somewhat less favorable social environments might be acceptable if they provide opportunities to travel outside of the area to more diverse places (however, this option may not be a sufficient compromise if you have a mate and/or children, unless they can travel with you as well). Thus be sure to negotiate resources such as possible research grants, conference travel support, and internal travel grant opportunities.

• *Assess departmental collegiality.* How well do your potential colleagues get along? Is there a sense of camaraderie and support in the department or program? These types of interactions may be determined during your onsite visit. A collegial environment on the academic front can help compensate for less than favorable conditions outside the institution. This is especially true because you may be more likely to forge close friendships with other academics. Thus a department of friendly individuals represents a potential pool of people not only for collaboration, but also for socializing. Talk with prospective peers and colleagues about lifestyle issues. If certain issues are important to you (e.g., religious diversity, racial/ethnic diversity), request to speak with other faculty members with your similar profile and interests. If this is not possible during your campus visit, ask your contact person for the e-mail addresses of people who are willing to talk with you about these issues. In addition, speak openly with your contact person. This person is usually interested in ensuring that your questions and concerns are addressed and may be more open to providing you with a candid assessment of the campus and local milieu. Also speak with senior faculty members in your graduate program. It may not seem so, but academia is a relatively small community—and disciplines are even smaller. Older faculty are often familiar with their past classmates and colleagues who are now employed at other institutions. They may also be familiar with incidents at any school you are interested in or know someone with helpful information. Again, you must determine the accuracy and veracity of any information provided, but don't overlook this valuable source of information.

• *Determine proximity to venues of interest.* Don't quickly dismiss a position because of its location. If you'd prefer to live in the city, but your only job offer is in a relatively small town, find out how far the location is from a city or regional social venues. Determine proximity by car as well as airplane. If you accept a position in an area with few social outlets, but in close proximity to such venues, you can still take advantage of them. This will also give you an opportunity to "get away" for a while. If you are thinking about accepting a position, but have concerns about your social life, consider traveling to more socially and culturally engaging places. However, this will require you to set aside funds (possibly on a monthly basis) to pay for such trips. For example, you may decide to take a short trip once each month. You may budget $75 each pay period for such trips (just as you would to pay your monthly bills). You can consider this travel your monthly "payment to yourself" for working hard. This option may be especially important for single candidates or those who are relocating to areas that are very different from their current place of residence. However, be sure not to isolate yourself. With a little effort, some degree of quality of life can be established in most places. A good place to begin is within your new department/program. Attempt to establish relationships with colleagues with whom you connect. And remember, a central source of commonality is the academic endeavor. Be willing to compromise. Consider the best balance between personal and professional issues. Again, no position will meet all of your professional and personal needs. The goal is to realistically determine the best balance for you and strive to locate a position that meets these goals. A willingness to compromise suggests a certain amount of flexibility on your part; understand that a successful academic search will require flexibility.

• *Plan community involvement.* No matter where you decide to relocate, plan to get involved in the community. Join the Rotary club or a local church. Plan to volunteer at a local center or seek membership on community boards. Plan to take part in events or join the YMCA or YWCA. By getting involved in the community, you increase your chances of establishing networks and finding friends and social partners, and ultimately increase the chances that certain personal needs will be met. You should also consider joining organizations that relate to your research interests.

Remember that you can teach and/or perform research at most institutions. While resources will vary and some positions will offer an array of perks that can facilitate your work, many institutions will have the basic resources you will need to teach and/or perform research. Yes, you will probably have to teach more courses at a small institution and budget your time carefully in the summer to perform research. And, yes, the publishing load will be greater at a larger institution and also require time-management skills of a different sort. But balancing the professional and personal arenas means realizing that, if you are unable to have a good quality of life in a given position, there are other academic institutions and options to consider. Always feel empowered to make a change.

9

Considerations for Nontraditional and Underrepresented Groups

I am reminded of the candidate who was courted by a progressive department involved in cutting-edge research in her area. The position seemed perfect, the academic package was replete with perks, and the location was somewhat isolated, but picturesque. However, the candidate did not consider any personal issues. And although her department is quite progressive, her lifestyle needs as a young, lesbian, biracial female are not being met. She is currently on the job market.

Just as a variety of personal issues that can affect your quality of life are linked to the academic and nonacademic climate, you must consider the influence of your individual traits on well-being and quality of life relative to a prospective position. You may have special considerations based on factors such as gender, race/ethnicity, age, marital status, sexual orientation, and family structure. All these factors may not be germane to you. However, those that are most important should be considered before you accept a position (and, in some instances, before you apply for one). This chapter focuses on issues that nontraditional and underrepresented candidates should consider as they attempt to balance professional and personal decisions during the employment search. Such candidates will have to consider many of the issues presented in Chapter 8 as well as those included here.

■ Your Personal Profile

• *Race/ethnicity/nationality.* While the majority of academics continue to be white males, racial and ethnic minorities are entering academia at growing rates. Research shows variations in representation by disciplines (e.g., Asian Americans in certain engineering fields, African Americans in education and sociology), but the trend suggests departments and programs should expect more racial/ethnic minorities to apply for positions. However, based on relatively low representation, members of such groups may have to address unique job search issues such as departmental receptivity to certain racial/ethnic–specific research interests, lack of critical mass on campus and in the community, and issues related to possibly being the first and only member of their group in the department or program. In addition, international candidates may have to contend with national, regional, and local cultural issues.

• *Gender.* Just as racial/ethnic candidates must assess quality of life issues based on cultural differences, female candidates may face challenges as members of predominantly male departments and programs.

• *Marital status.* As noted earlier, married candidates must examine a potential position based on their needs and those of their mates. In addition, single candidates should also consider the implications of accepting certain positions in terms of availability of other single people for friendship and dating and social outlets that cater to single lifestyles.

• *Family structure.* Your personal interest in a position may also be influenced by family structure. Family statuses such as single parent, divorced with children, married with children, or single and living alone can affect your viewpoint about the attractiveness of a position.

• *Religion.* The availability of synagogues, mosques, black churches or parishes (or lack thereof) can greatly influence quality of life. For some, a position in a locale without their preferred place of worship may not be a position they can consider.

• *Sexual orientation.* Just as unmarried people may directly or indirectly consider the availability of other unmarried people in a prospective area, some candidates who are gay or lesbian may be influenced by the perception that a prospective community lacks other gays and lesbians with whom to socialize and date. In addition, the receptivity and tolerance of a community to sexual diversity may also be a concern.

• *Region.* Candidates who prefer to live in a specific region (i.e., north, south, east, west, mid-west), should decide how open they are to relocating to a different region and what such a move may mean for their quality of life. For example, if you have always lived in New York, it may be difficult to get used to life in Montana—no matter how great the job offer.

• *Social setting (town or city).* And just as region may be important, if you are accustomed to life in a big city, rural life may not be an option. In contrast, if you prefer to live in a rural area, the crowds and hustle and bustle of a large city may not be attractive. Your ideal position at an impressive institution may be located in a less than favorable area (e.g., that top Research I institution located in a small, isolated, rural community, or a comprehensive liberal arts school located in an impoverished urban center). You must weigh the options to determine whether you will be able to adjust in a setting if it differs dramatically from your current or preferred social setting.

• *Life course status.* Quality of life issues may differ based on your life course status. Slightly older candidates entering academia as a second career will have different needs than younger, newly minted Ph.D.s. Females of childbearing age will have different considerations than older females and males.

Only you can determine what these identities mean to you, their importance relative to your quality of life, and whether and how they influence the positions you consider. For example, decide whether you need or want to live in close proximity to a specific ethnic community or simply have access to one nearby. How do these factors weigh relative to your career trajectory, that is, would you be willing to trade the absence of certain social or cultural resources in order to get a position at a Research I institution or would you be willing to trade such a position for a post at a teaching college in a diverse, bustling city? Given the importance of this topic, it is addressed at length in subsequent sections.

• *Intersecting issues.* When assessing potential quality of life relative to prospective positions, some candidates must consider a variety of issues simultaneously and they may face a unique set of needs and challenges. In general, the more varied your personal traits, the more issues you may want to consider. For example, quality of life concerns will undoubtedly be different for a candidate who is a married, white male as compared to an unmarried female from India. And their needs will differ from those of a married, Asian female with two small children, or those of a candidate who is Hispanic, gay, and a single parent. And females of childbearing age, those who are pregnant, or who are rearing children should assess issues relative to gender, family structure, and life course. While each candidate is an academic, searching for a tenure-track position and (quite possibly) vying for the same position, some of them must consider a wider variety of quality of life issues if they want to increase their chances of finding a position that is both professionally and personally rewarding.

In general, the more unique or distinct your personal traits, the smaller the available social subgroup will likely exist in a given community. For many, this challenge can be rectified by simply locating a position in a large city (or near one). However, there are only so many such positions available and you are not guaranteed a post. This means that you may have to compromise and that some of your personal needs may not be met. And minority candidates who may wish to live in a city should consider other options such as posts in larger college towns or satellite campuses, regional locations, or positions in rural areas that are in close proximity to cities.

As mentioned earlier, membership in a particular minority group does not automatically mean that you will have to consider these personal issues. For example, for some candidates, race/ethnicity may not be a point of concern when assessing quality of life relative to a prospective position. For others, it may be one of the most important concerns. For some, religion is secondary, for others, it is primary. You will have to determine what your "nontraditional or underrepresented" status means to you, its place of importance in the search process, and whether and how to best consider it in your deliberations.

■ Maximizing Your Options: Suggestions to Consider and Questions to Ask

Here are some issues and questions that nontraditional candidates and those from underrepresented groups should consider during the campus visit or before they accept a position. You will note that some of the questions and issues are personal as well as professional. This is the case because, for nontraditional and underrepresented candidates, especially those considering positions at predominately white institutions, personal and professional issues are closely connected. It is important to identify and detail the issues (including strengths and drawbacks) relative to a position and to rank those issues that are most important to you. The goal is to make as informed a decision as possible and locate a post that represents the best professional and personal fit for you.

The Importance of Intentionality

If an offer seems too good to be sure, it probably is. Beware of "schools bearing gifts." While you should expect an employment package reflective of both the current salary and perks in your industry and your unique skills, talent, and experience, be skeptical of offers that greatly exceed your expectations. Make sure there aren't ulterior motives. Does the department seem genuinely interested in you or simply interested in filling the position with a female candidate? Have female candidates been recruited in the past only to work six years and fail to get tenure? Is the enticing package an attempt to recruit you into an unhealthy work climate? You may not know all the answers to such questions, but follow your instincts. This type of approach should rarely occur because it undermines a department economically and is unethical, but it can happen.

In order to avoid being drawn into a position that may prove to be a poor fit both professionally and personally, it is important to have a broad idea of your career plans. When considering a career path it is important to realize that there are a variety of paths (e.g., a comprehensive liberal arts institution, teaching college, Big 10 University, Research II institution) that are appropriate and acceptable based on your needs, goals, and lifestyle. For some, it may be best to begin a career at a smaller institution and work your way up to a larger institution. Others may choose to compete for positions at larger institutions at the outset or focus on smaller institutions in general. You may wish to focus on teaching and mentoring students while others are more interested in establishing a publishing career and locating external funding. Consider historically black colleges and universities (HBCUs) or specialty schools. Institutions that have traditionally served a particular segment of the population may provide excellent opportunities to engage in teaching, research, and also feel connected to a specific cultural community. Apply to a women's or men's college, a seminary, a teaching college, or a joint appointment at an institution with an urban research center. Think about creative ways to mesh your personal aspirations with academic work that is also personally meaningful.

Define Important Concepts and Consider Their Implications

What exactly does "minority" mean at the prospective institution? This concept can be defined in a variety of ways and it is important to understand the institution's definition as you review their hiring and retention data. Do they distinguish between categories such as gender, race, ethnicity, and national origin? How does the institution "count" females who are also members of racial/ethnic groups? Are Asian and Hispanic faculty considered minorities or white? Are Africans grouped with African Americans? Different institutions may have different definitions. Nontraditional definitions may mask underrepresentation of certain groups and suggest overrepresentation of others.

Also determine the meaning and importance of "diversity." Diversity is one of the new buzzwords in academia (as is multiculturalism). Many institutions are attempting to diversify or create diversity on campus. Find out what this term means at the prospective institution. Is the term linked specifically to race/ethnicity? Does it include other measures of culture? Determine whether a diversity initiative is part of the institution's strategies and goals and whether resources have been allocated to bring about and/or maintain diversity? Is such a plan evident at the departmental/program level? Does the institution realize and acknowledge the benefits of having a diverse, multicultural faculty, staff, and student body? Determine the specific plans that are implemented to recruit various minority applicants and the types of economic resources and personnel committed to this task. In general, institutions that budget funds and personnel to recruit such faculty and staff (and students) place a stronger emphasis on diversity.

Although you may have initially considered the minority mix at a certain institution from a professional perspective, revisit it for personal reasons. Is the minority population in the department/program primarily assistant professors? Associate professors? Or are there several full professors in the unit? Do women and racial/ethnic minorities hold administrative posts such as department chairperson, assistant or associate dean, dean, or provost? Are low numbers due to retention problems or an unfriendly climate? The presence of senior faculty members from diverse groups suggests that people are not hindered from tenure and promotion by issues such as sexism and racism, and bodes well that your successful progress in teaching/research will be rewarded and interests in transitioning into administration are feasible.

It will also be important to determine whether a critical mass exists or whether attempts are being made to create one. A critical mass refers to a sufficient number of people in a setting to constitute a group. One female colleague in a department does not represent a critical mass (unless it is a department of 2 to 3 people). Having a critical mass may be important professionally and personally. Such a group may provide social support, prevent isolation, help minimize relocation challenges, and possibly link you to a diverse community outside of academia. For reasons such as limited graduates, competition from other institutions, retention problems, and past negative climates, many institutions will not have a critical mass of certain groups. You must decide whether such a group is important. In addition, determine whether the department/program would like to create a critical mass, that is, are there plans to hire more faculty from nontraditional and underrepresented groups and, if so, what is the projected plan? Institutions with homogeneous faculty may be in the process of recruiting nontraditional and underrepresented groups. This may suggest a willingness to diversify.

If possible, determine hiring and retention rates for nontraditional and underrepresented groups. During your campus visit, ask the department head/chairperson for the statistics on hiring and retention. In some cases, these data are available via the affirmative action department. This information will help you determine hiring and retention patterns for the institution in general, and for your prospective department/program in particular. Consistent turnover and failure to hire members from such groups may be a subtle sign of an unhealthy climate.

Interactions with Diverse Groups

Talk with people who currently work in the prospective department/program about the climate, their transition period and process, and any challenges they've faced. Ask for their candid opinions about the institution and the community. People who have had negative experiences may be open to warning you about potential problems. For example, I'm reminded of a candidate who was contacted by a department member after his onsite interview. The faculty member informed the candidate that, although a variety of people had been hired, the department had never tenured a racial/ethnic minority—in its entire history. This current faculty member had just been rejected for tenure (although he felt he met the academic requirements) and felt strongly about warning other racial/ethnic minorities. Some might consider the faculty member merely a disgruntled employee; however, although the candidate was offered a position, he elected to accept a post elsewhere.

Specifically, ask for time during your campus visit to meet with *diverse* senior faculty. Many departments will schedule sessions with representatives from racial/ethnic and other minority groups when a candidate is a member of a minority group. If this is not done, request such sessions. During the talk, focus on what they say as well as what they *don't* say. This includes gestures, the tendency to avoid questions of race, gender, sexual orientation, and class, evasive responses or responses you feel are "politically correct." In addition, do they appear downtrodden, alienated, or uncomfortable? You must decide what to do with their feedback and, in some cases, you may not know how to accurately interpret their responses. In some cases, faculty members will be quite candid with their feedback, insight, and suggestions. And if you feel uncomfortable about the climate, follow your instincts. If an institution does not have *any* senior faculty from diverse groups, this is important information for you to note as well. However, don't assume minority-based allegiances. It is presumptuous to assume that issues of diversity are important to potential colleagues who are members of minority groups just because they are important to you. For example, don't expect commonalities with a Cuban department member just because you and he are Cuban.

Attempt to locate campus multicultural facilities. Find out whether the campus houses a multicultural center, gay and lesbian network, a black cultural center, specialty libraries, or libraries that house ethnic books, journals, and artifacts. Does the campus offer special services, activities, organizations, or gathering places for students and faculty of color? Is there a Women's Caucus or Latino Caucus on campus or other organizations that provide services for nontraditional or underrepresented faculty and staff? These types of facilities can serve as outlets for faculty who may feel isolated in their departments and suggests a presence of such groups on campus. Also ask about multicultural venues in nearby locales. As mentioned in Chapter 8, don't reject a good post simply due to its locale. Consider other options. For example, a single African American male accepted a position that was great for him—but the institution is located in a small town with little diversity or nightlife. However, the town is 45 minutes by car from a large diverse city and less than one hour's airplane trip (via a relatively inexpensive local carrier) from several other large urban centers. So he spends the week focusing on teaching and research and schedules weekend excursions to more socially diverse settings. Using this approach, he was also able to publish aggressively, get strong teaching evaluations, and ultimately earn early tenure.

Even if minority representation is minimal on campus, assess whether a minority community exists. Is there an ethnic enclave in the area? Is there a black community? A Jewish community? Do Asian residents live in a certain area of the town? You may want to determine whether a specific community exists as a possible source of social networks, support, and cultural resources.

Determine the extent of goods and services for minority groups. Are there ethnic stores in the prospective city or town? Is there a beauty shop that specializes in black hair care or a dermatologist that specializes in black skin care? What types of radio broadcasts are available? Are there Spanish-speaking, Korean, Rhythm & Blues, and Soul broadcasts? Are there specialty restaurants? Answers to these types of questions will be important in gauging whether you will have the necessary practical resources to maintain a positive quality of life. For example, a female, African American classmate of mine relocated to a small rural area. Having lived in a predominately black community, she was accustomed to getting medical service from a female, African American physician. Although she tried several local doctors, she finally opted to use a local physician for emergencies only, and established her primary care with an African American doctor in a city 45 minutes away. She travels to the city for physicals and other major healthcare needs. Some might consider this an unnecessary effort, but it was extremely important for her to have her healthcare needs addressed by someone with whom she felt most comfortable. She considered this a small price to pay for locating a good academic position and meeting her personal healthcare needs.

Lastly, racial/ethnic minorities and females may be expected to ask questions about the presence or absence of group members on campus, in the prospective department, or in the community. However, other issues related to your age, marital status, or sexual orientation, are typically avoided for legal reasons (questions about mates can be addressed by candidates if they initiate queries or after a position is accepted). These issues may be important to you, but you will not be able to ask direct questions about them. However, look for other signs of diversity that may suggest a progressive climate.

Family Considerations

Although quality of life issues for mates and children were mentioned in Chapter 8, it is particularly important for nontraditional or underrepresented candidates. Just as you should examine issues of diversity, cultural climate, social support, and cultural networks for yourself, it is imperative to consider what relocation may mean for mates and children. You may be able to adjust to circumstances much easier and more quickly than, say, your children. Children in their formative years may experience isolation and face racial/ethnic or cultural identity concerns. This may be a special challenge if your family has lived in a more diverse area or in an area where your group was in the majority (such as an ethnic enclave). *This cannot be stressed enough!* Be sure to include significant others in your decision about a position and attempt to identify and address their concerns. In addition, also realize that support within your family will undoubtedly make any relocation effort more inviting.

Female candidates who are pregnant or plan to become pregnant in the near future should attempt to identify the primary issues related to the impending changes in their personal and professional lives. You are not required to notify a prospective institution of a pregnancy or short-term plans and institutions cannot legally view your candidacy negatively if you are pregnant. However, it is important to consider your options because they can dramatically influence your family life and career—and because once you have accepted a tenure-track post, you will be expected to fulfill the responsibilities of the post. If you are already pregnant you may choose to remain on the market to locate a tenure-track position and attempt to balance these new areas of your life. Or you could opt to take a post without a "tenure clock" until after the baby's birth and search for a tenure-track post the following year. Such decisions will be based on your professional and personal goals. Although you will get varying opinions, seek advice from female academics who are attempting to balance research and/or teaching and childrearing. If you choose to seek a tenure-track position, rely on resources and observation to help identify institutions that may be more family friendly for employed mothers. This means asking female faculty at your current institution for possible feedback about institutions in which you are interested, reviewing institutional web sites for the number of female faculty who appear to be of childbearing age, and, during onsite visits, trying to assess the number of females of childbearing age in prospective or related departments. These strategies will not provide hard data but they may help you gauge institutional culture.

Also be sure to consider the broad drawbacks and/or benefits relative to marital status, age, race/ethnicity, and culture. Nontraditional and underrepresented groups must contend with low representation on campus and in the community. These effects are often compounded if you are unmarried. For example, a single, Jewish female who is interested in dating males within her faith will face dating challenges if she accepts a position at a campus with few single, Jewish male employees in an area with few single, Jewish male residents. Members of other racial/ethnic groups may experience similar situations. If some type of resolution is not made (a compromise in terms of dating outside her faith or establishing long-distance relationships), the benefits of her academic career may be diminished by her limited dating options and loneliness. Single candidates must consider the implications of their relationship status before accepting a position (especially in rural regions); for single people who are also members of other minority groups, this is especially important.

Proactive Personal Options to Foster Diversity

If you are a member of a relatively homogeneous institution, department, or program, consider creative options to expose yourself to diversity. Some options include joint appointments, affiliated status, and involvement in diverse academic organizations. A joint appointment (such as political science and women's studies, or sociology and Asian studies) may enable you to focus research and teaching in your areas of interest and also interact and collaborate with a diverse group of faculty members or people from your specific minority group. Some disciplines lend themselves better to joint posts than others (e.g., arts and sciences). Some institutions have joint relationships in place; others may not, but may be open to considering such options. If such positions don't currently exist, talk with the department head/chairperson about the possibility of such an arrangement (if not at the time of appointment, to be considered later). However, realize that joint appointments, if not organized properly and made part of the formal and informal milieu of an institution, can result in negative experiences because of conflicting expectations, undue demands on one's time, and unclear tenure expectations.

If you are interested in becoming joint appointed, but this option is not available, request to become an affiliated faculty member with another department or program. For example, as a candidate of Asian descent, you may accept a position in the history department but also become an affiliated faculty member in the Asian studies program. An affiliated faculty member establishes a connection with another department/program and is able to participate in certain functions in that unit (as determined by that unit). Affiliated status typically occurs after meeting certain requirements determined by the department or program in which you are interested (for example, agreement to teach a course every three years, cross-listing your courses, or taking part in certain programs and events). This option will enable you to be actively involved in another more diverse unit even if a joint appointment is not possible.

Membership in group-specific organizations and conferences can also enhance your career and experiences. These memberships can provide opportunities to network, establish (perhaps only weak) social ties, and develop a critical mass of colleagues from a particular group. Organizations exist across most disciplines including the social sciences and liberal arts areas such as sociology, political science, communications, psychology, and cultural studies, as well as engineering, computer programming, and mathematics. In addition to group-specific organizations, many national conferences also maintain subsections that lend themselves to diverse representation. A few group-specific organizations include: the Association of Black Sociologists, the Association of Hispanic Professionals, the College Language Association, the American Association of University Women, the National Association of Mathematicians, the National Society of Black Engineers, Sociologists for Women in Society, and the Association of Black Psychologists. In addition, annual meetings provide an opportunity to meet scholars, locate peers for collaboration, and just have fun.

Junior faculty members are often encouraged to generate single-authored publications to show their unique contribution to the literature in their discipline. And while this should be your goal, it may be equally important to take part in interdisciplinary research. Diverse research teams benefit not only from group efforts, but from varied methodologies and techniques as well. In addition, collaboration can help maintain connections with peers from graduate school, and allow you to efficiently tackle research projects and increase your publishing efforts. And just as group-specific organizations provide you with access to peers from specific racial, ethnic, or gender groups, applied and/or activist-oriented organizations provide opportunities to engage with peers and others who may share your interests in applied work and issues such as social policy, community empowerment, and practical application of academic findings. Such organizations are often found in the social sciences (e.g., the Society for the Study of Social Problems) or associated with community-based organizations.

Last, if possible, attempt to locate funds to recruit diverse undergraduate and graduate students. Even if the faculty in a given department or program is relatively homogeneous, the student body may be more diverse. Find out the number and percentage of undergraduate and graduate students in the program from nontraditional (e.g., students entering second careers) and underrepresented groups. If numbers are low, try to negotiate resources (through the department or in collaboration with campus recruitment) for recruiting diverse students. For example, an African American colleague in psychology negotiated her contract to include funds for travel and recruitment of students from HBCUs for graduate school and to specifically work with her in her lab. She was able to justify such efforts because they would directly aid in her research and also enhance diversity in a relatively homogeneous department. Such efforts may provide a mixture of graduate students for mentoring and collaboration or a critical mass of students to help enhance diversity.

Negotiating Campus Life

Most candidates from nontraditional or underrepresented groups attended graduate programs where they were also in the minority. You may have been the only female in your cohort or the only Latino in a graduate program. Reflect on that process and the strategies you used to be successful there. Recall the techniques, skills, and approaches you used to earn your Ph.D. These same skills will be needed to locate a position, establish a career, earn tenure, and make a contribution to your discipline. Being able to rely on past experiences will help you establish your career in any setting. Also be able to honestly assess your strengths and growth areas. Given your exposure to an entire campus of faculty, staff, and students, you will undoubtedly experience some negative encounters that you should address directly and professionally. However, be careful not to allow such encounters to taint your view of others so that you are automatically suspicious of them. Be able to distinguish between unfounded comments and constructive advice, especially from mentors or supportive senior colleagues. This means being able to objectively and honestly examine your strong points as a researcher and teacher as well as areas that need improvement. This means working toward meeting and exceeding the requirements for milestones such as tenure and promotion, asking for assistance if you need it, and learning to negotiate faculty, staff, and student interactions.

Students who attend institutions with a diverse faculty are accustomed to instruction from a diverse staff. However, if you are considering a post at an institution that is relatively homogeneous, many of the students may not have had a nonwhite or female professor (some students from rural communities may never have interacted closely with nonwhites). Expect responses ranging from curious interest to disdain. Some students will be open to learning, no matter the professor, while others will have difficulty taking direction from a minority member (especially female minority faculty). Others may challenge your credibility and some may assume the course will be easy. Still others may be skeptical about speaking in class for fear of making inappropriate comments or statements that might make them appear to be a bigot (this fear may arise if you are teaching controversial or sensitive topics such as racism, slavery, the Holocaust, or sexism).

Also expect varied responses from minority students. For example, if you are Cuban American, some Cuban American students will consider you a welcome change and be excited about your presence, some may feel that you will give them special concessions, and still others who are not Cuban-identified, may attempt to distance themselves from you. And some students may believe your minority status makes you a biased instructor when teaching certain courses (e.g., a Latino teaching a course on race/ethnicity or a female teaching a course on women's issues). Regardless of the response, it is important to establish your position as the professor and the course standard early on. Also strive to create and maintain an open, professional climate that is conducive to nonthreatening discussion and critical thinking. Most students will eventually accept you (although you can expect interesting comments on your course evaluations from time to time). Those who cannot accept you will typically drop the course.

Be intentional about addressing time-management issues. As a member of a nontraditional or underrepresented group, you will be called upon to take on many responsibilities in your new position. This is especially true if you are entering an institution or department/program with little diversity. You will be asked to serve on committees to improve diversity, provide input to campus groups that wish to consider the "minority experience," and spearhead diversity initiatives. In addition, you will be a magnet for students from your underrepresented group in need of mentoring, academic advice, social support, and, in some cases, a friendly face (remember that you will have to provide such support to nonminority students in your classes and department as well). In addition, you may be asked to serve on community and local boards and organizations.

Given these tasks, you will be pulled in many directions. If you do not manage your time properly, you will become overwhelmed and possibly burn out. Your ability to effectively teach and perform research will be undermined as well. I was told the story of a Hispanic junior faculty member who found herself in such a predicament—teaching, mentoring students of Hispanic descent as well as non-Hispanic students, serving as the adviser for a campus sorority, and spearheading a student rap session on social issues—not to mention her nonacademic duties. Needless to say, she was unable to find time to perform the research needed to get tenure. So although she provided important teaching and services within the the institution and the larger community, she did not publish, and she suffered the consequences. The lesson here is to learn to prioritize requirements for academic success, manage your time wisely, balance the professional and personal, and, most important, learn to say no.

The Reality of Social Ills

You can expect to encounter "ism" at even the most liberal, progressive institution. Racism, sexism, homophobia, classism, and ageism still exist. The more progressive institutions do not condone such attitudes and behavior and may work concertedly to cultivate a multicultural environment. Other institutions will have a more unfriendly climate. In addition, tolerance on campus may not transfer offsite. Be aware of these types of social ills and how they can affect your professional as well as personal life. And while you realize that you will encounter people with these types of sentiments, also realize that you do not have to accept their behavior. Also realize the reality of statistics. In general, the graduation rates for underrepresented groups with Ph.D.s are low. Of those, many may be in great demand, so subsequently only a few may accept positions at your institution of interest. In addition, due to dynamics such as supply and demand in your discipline and quality of life issues, a certain degree of turnover is likely to occur. Yet *you* can represent change. If you are considering a position at a place where you will be "the first" or the "only," also consider it an opportunity to help enhance and expand the culture at the institution in general and the department/program in particular. An infusion of diverse faculty members gradually diversifies institutions, departments, or programs, as well as local communities. This will also change the climate as new faculty provide input and contribute to the overall climate. Yes, it may get lonely sometimes (and be sure to consider this possibility) as a sole representative in a unit, but change often occurs gradually.

10

Returning to the Job Market:
The Pre-Tenure Search

Although much of this book focuses on preparing graduate students to enter and successfully negotiate the academic job market, it is important to consider the experiences and challenges of people who re-enter the job market before receiving tenure in their current position. This chapter focuses on the job search process for people (often referred to as "junior faculty") who are re-entering the job market pre-tenure. You may have been employed in a tenure-track position for several years, but have decided that the post is not a good fit, personally and/or professionally. Reasons may vary, but you may decide to re-enter the job market before being considered for tenure at your current institution. Many of your experiences while interviewing as a graduate student will still apply as a junior faculty member on the job market again. However, because you are applying for a somewhat different post (and you are not a traditional applicant), certain aspects of the job search will differ. This chapter covers issues to be considered for people in the early stages of their academic career who are contemplating re-entering the academic job market.

■ Why Re-Enter the Job Market:
The Second Time Around

The reasons for re-entering the job arena may be professional or personal—or both. For example, you may enjoy your current position in terms of professional development, but find that the locale does not meet your personal needs. Or you may enjoy the social life afforded by the area, but have realized that you would prefer a position at a teaching college or a larger urban university. Whatever your reasons, it is important to objectively assess them and weigh your concerns alongside the potential time and energy required to begin another employment search. If you have only held your current post a short time (for example, one or two years), have you given yourself sufficient time to determine the benefits and drawbacks of remaining there versus re-entering the job market? Are your concerns objective (for example, the teaching load prevents you from taking part in research) or largely subjective (you don't "like" the department head)? Are your concerns institutionally systemic (the former scenario) or potentially short-lived (the latter one)?

It is important to specifically determine the reasons for considering re-entering the job market, the pros and cons of such a move (developing a list for each would be time well spent), and whether you have the time and energy to perform another employment search. However, re-entering the job market differs from your search during graduate school because you will now have to search for a new position while *simultaneously* performing your current one. And although graduate school was hectic and busy, your current position is probably even more so. Once you decide to seek another position, you should develop a process that maximizes the employment search, but not at the expense of your current teaching and/or research agenda. Having an employment search plan will help facilitate the process (refer to Chapters 4, 6, and 7, and information below). But before you decide to re-enter the employment arena, you should weigh your options. A list of some possible benefits and drawbacks are provided below to assist in a reflective decisionmaking process. It is crucial to complete this process so that you can make the most informed decision possible. Only you can decide whether re-entering the market is best for you.

Potential Benefits of Re-Entering the Job Market
- A position that is a better professional and/or personal fit
- Ability to use existing knowledge from previous job search to facilitate the new one

- Ability to establish professional and/or personal roots in a more suitable place
- Improved quality of life
- New colleagues and friends
- Increased salary and benefits
- Expanded social network (current colleagues and new ones)
- No longer "wasting time" in a seemingly fruitless position
- May make more knowledgeable, informed job decision the second time around
- The excitement of an unfamiliar, new environment
- Benefits for significant others (spouse, partner and/or children)

Potential Drawbacks of Re-Entering the Job Market
- Inability to locate another position
- Time and energy required to perform a thorough job search
- Possibility of moving to a more problematic, negative professional and/or personal environment
- Loss of work time at current position
- Loss of current colleagues and friends
- Need to establish credibility and status in a new department or program
- Need to develop new collegial relationships and friends
- Alienation of colleagues in your current department
- Possibility of having to re-start the "tenure clock"
- Discomfort associated with an unfamiliar, new environment
- Drawbacks for significant others (spouse, partner and/or children)

You may be able to identify other potential benefits and drawbacks specific to your situation. Try to think of as many issues as possible and rank each (include significant others in the thought process because they will be affected by your decision as well). The pros should outnumber (and outweigh) the cons. And the objective of the next search is to minimize these possible drawbacks and maximize potential benefits (again, this will vary for each individual), which may differ from some of the issues you considered during your first search. However, realize that certain concerns may override others (for example, for some people, no amount of professional success can make up for an unfulfilled personal life). Attempt to assess each issue objectively, acknowledging those issues that should be considered somewhat more subjectively. Also realize that it will be impossible to be 100 percent certain about the decision of whether or not to re-enter the job market—you can only be as informed as possible. However, once you have assessed the potential benefits and drawbacks and have decided to re-enter the market, proceed with confidence and expedience. The following sections address important next steps.

■ Timing and Profile Positioning

It is important to determine *when* you plan to re-enter the job market. The search process for someone who has held their current position one or two years will be somewhat different from a junior faculty member who is in, say, year five or the penultimate year (i.e., year six, the year a tenure-track faculty member will automatically be considered for tenure). Are you planning to position yourself as a "new" assistant professor? An advanced assistant professor? Or are you planning to compete for positions as an associate professor? This decision, which I refer to as "profile positioning" is crucial, because it will shape the type of cover letter you write and how you present your professional teaching and/or research experiences to prospective search committees. In general, if you have only held your current position one to two years, because of your limited teaching and/or research experiences, you may want to position yourself as a "new" assistant professor and apply for such positions.

The closer you are to year six, the better chance you will have to compete for either an advanced assistant professor or associate professor post—*if* you have been productive (this latter caveat will be examined in more detail shortly). However, some assistant professors opt to "start all over" no matter how long they have held their current position. That is a decision each individual must make. Be mindful, no matter what profile you select (for example, you have been an assistant professor for five years and plan to apply for associate professor positions), it will then be your responsibility to convince prospective search committees that you are a match for that post. Also remember that some institutions limit the number of years you can credit toward tenure if you are currently five years into your career.

Views differ among senior faculty about the pros and cons of re-entering the job market before tenure. Some people believe that, if you are going to locate another tenure-track position, it is best to do so before getting tenure at your current institution because there tend to be more available positions for assistant professors than for associate professors. According to this premise, it is better to re-enter the job market sooner rather than later (for example, before the third-year review). Others suggest that competing for a position as either an associate professor or an advanced assistant professor can provide more negotiating leverage that may result in a higher salary and more attractive package. Supporters of the latter camp would encourage junior faculty to re-enter the job market either after earning tenure or in year five or six of their current position.

There are potential benefits and drawbacks for both viewpoints. Although you must decide what is best for you, it is important to consider timing in order to maximize the potential for locating another position most suited for you professionally and personally. If you are a more advanced assistant professor, it may also be prudent to leverage your search by applying for positions as both an assistant and associate professor. In each instance, your profile position would differ. For example, once you obtain an interview for an assistant professor position, you must convince the search committee of your credibility as an advanced assistant professor and how they would benefit by selecting you rather than hiring a graduating Ph.D. or ABD. In the latter instance, you must convince the search committee that, although you have not earned tenure, your research and/or teaching merit an associate's rank.

I noted the importance of productivity earlier. Deciding whether and when to re-enter the job market and how to position yourself will be largely shaped by academic productivity. Regardless of whether you are applying for a research position, teaching position, or a combination, it will be necessary to have the credentials to be considered a viable candidate. How many publications do you have? In what types of journals? Do you have strong teaching evaluations? Have you been able to secure internal and/or external grants? The exact definition of productivity will vary based on the type of institutions to which you are applying, but most search committees will be interested in research and teaching performance. For example, if you've held your current position at a public, four-year, Research I institution for more than four years, you may be expected to have at least 5 publications in appropriate peer-reviewed journals in your discipline and strong teaching evaluations as compared to a candidate who has only been in the post one or two years.

If your productivity has been somewhat low (a good benchmark would be to gauge whether your current progress, if continued at the same pace, would make you a strong, viable candidate for tenure at your current institution), you may wish to apply for assistant professor positions or wait another academic year until your productivity makes you more competitive before re-entering the market. On the other hand, if you have been very productive (i.e., numerous publications, grants, and strong teaching evaluations), you have a better chance of positioning yourself either as an advanced assistant professor or possibly competing successfully for an associate professor's position. It is important to objectively examine your current vita and teaching record and compare your profile with respective advertisements (refer to strategies to maximize the use of the cover letter below). You should also attempt to gauge how and when your current productivity profile may change (for example, do you have several "revise and resubmit" articles or a grant pending, or do you believe the teaching evaluations for your current courses will be more favorable than in the past) to determine whether and when you should re-enter the job arena and exactly how you should position yourself.

■ The Cover Letter

The cover letter for candidates re-entering the job market is often more crucial than for graduate students applying for initial positions. The cover letter provides an opportunity to justify re-entry, position your profile, address possible shortcomings in productivity, and generally convince a search committee that you are the ideal candidate for the post. As illustrated in Chapter 4, different formats should be used depending on whether you are applying for a teaching or a research position. As a current junior faculty member, your cover letter will include one piece of information not available for graduate students who are entering the market—the fact that you currently hold a tenure-track position. This information is important because it provides an automatic signal to a search committee that your academic profile while in graduate school was strong enough to garner a similar post—and will usually increase your stature relative to ABDs and new Ph.D.s entering the market. That you currently hold an academic position also suggests your transition into a new position at their institution may not be as challenging or time consuming as for ABDs and new Ph.D.s.

The cover letter should follow the format suggested in the examples in Chapter 4—with some revisions. Be sure to reference your current tenure-track position in the first paragraph as well as your interest and excitement about possibly interviewing at their institution. The first paragraph should also broadly reference your research and teaching subjects and the exact post to which you are applying (i.e., profile positioning). If you are currently an assistant professor, but are applying for a position as an associate professor, clearly note this in the first paragraph as well as your intention to both justify why you should be considered for the position and provide subsequent supporting documentation.

The cover letter should also broadly explain why you are re-entering the market. This information should be presented diplomatically—and emphasize the desire to join their department, rather than the desire to leave your current post. Even if your decision is largely personal, you should focus on academic reasons for wishing to join their department. Does their department have more faculty members who perform similar research in your area of interest? Are you excited about increased opportunities to focus on teaching and mentoring students? Would you prefer a post that focuses more on traditional research? Do you think that your research and teaching interests would be best suited to a large, public institution? These types of reasons for re-entering the job market are acceptable and can help address important questions for a search committee while simultaneously presenting you positively. Avoid making negative remarks about your existing position or department because it suggests that you may not be a team player or that you may be attempting to leave your current post under less than ideal circumstances. If you are interested in leaving your current post because of quality of life issues, views vary about whether to disclose this information. I recommend focusing on academic issues and your desire to continue your career at this new institution.

The next paragraphs of the cover letter should specifically highlight current research projects, journal articles, and any special publishing accomplishments. For example, if you have published in a premier journal in your discipline, this should be noted. It is important to provide details about your research efforts, methods, findings, and contributions to the larger body of research in your discipline. This information provides evidence that you have already begun to perform successfully in an academic capacity. Be sure to associate each research topic with publications and/or grants (only focus on publications in print, forthcoming, or under review) so that a search committee can make direct links between your research interests and your ability to successfully complete research endeavors. Grants (internal and external) and fellowships (for example, if you are a Fulbright recipient) should also be noted here as an indicator of your commitment to obtain outside funding and excel as an academician. These paragraphs should also *specifically* illustrate why a candidate with research experience such as yourself would be an ideal fit for *their* department. Such details are crucial in order to distinguish yourself from other candidates (particularly if you are an assistant professor applying for a position as an associate professor).

The cover letter should detail teaching performance. This includes the type and number of courses taught (include any graduate courses, if applicable), performance ratings, and how such courses would benefit their department or program. Comparative departmental performance ratings would also be beneficial. Be sure to highlight courses you developed, why you did so, and how they have enhanced the curriculum at your current institution. This section should also include advanced courses or flagship classes you have taught (because some institutions only allow senior faculty to teach such classes, this may be impressive to the committee). Include a brief reference to conferences where you have presented and sessions you have organized. Also note your involvement on or leadership in student research committees, master's theses or dissertation committees, or any special student mentoring you have provided. This information is especially important if you are applying for a teaching post. Remind the reader of your ability to successfully balance your teaching and research responsibilities in your current position. If you are applying for a teaching post that de-emphasizes traditional research, provide information about your teaching credentials *first,* followed by a somewhat abbreviated presentation of your research interests. In contrast, note that most institutions that require research also require stellar teaching—so be sure to emphasize both areas of your academic profile.

Note that the suggested vita format in Chapter 4 is still appropriate. However, references to dissertation work will be replaced with information about your current research activity. The vita should be updated to reflect your research and teaching experiences in your current position. Information from your graduate stint can be referenced, but not at the expense of the focus on your work as a tenure-track assistant professor. Clearly identify publications, grants, and other scholarly accomplishments as well as teaching-related accolades. Furthermore, focus on courses you have taught rather than those you would like to teach and be sure to update the contact information of your references if they have changed. Be sure that your current vita highlights your accomplishments since obtaining a tenure-track post. This information will reinforce your acceptability as a candidate among the search committee members.

■ Letters of Recommendation

As was the case with the job search while in graduate school, most institutions will still require three or four letters of recommendation. To expedite the application process, some institutions initially only require contact information about potential references—such people would be contacted after a large applicant pool has been reduced to a set of the most acceptable candidates. Other institutions will not consider an application packet complete without letters of recommendation. Yet soliciting letters of recommendation if you are re-entering the market can be a bit challenging. In many instances, people most knowledgeable about your performance to date are also employed at the institution you plan to leave. Also, you may not want people in your department to know that you are on the job market again. Thus confidentiality is crucial. So who should you ask to write letters on your behalf?

As was the case when you were competing for your current position, you want to solicit people who can provide strong letters of recommendation for you—a suspiciously short, vague, or lukewarm letter is often as damaging as no letter at all. A letter from a leading scholar or master teaching in your discipline would also be beneficial. Because you may not be able to request letters from members of your current department (many committees would not expect you to), potentially acceptable candidates include members of your dissertation committee or senior scholars in your field with whom you may have established close ties via annual conferences or during collaborative research projects.

In some instances, you may have a trusted senior colleague in your department who can write a letter of reference for you *and* maintain confidentiality. However, the decision to divulge that you are on the job market again to someone in your immediate department should be made cautiously. Remember, even people with good intentions may inadvertently slip and soon the entire department may know of your plans. Although you are potentially looking for another post, you don't know whether your search will be successful—and it is important to avoid alienating existing colleagues should you have to remain at your current post longer than anticipated. However, you can creatively tap into existing relationships at your current institution. For example, although a colleague of mine did not request letters of reference from people in his immediate department, he had developed strong ties with several full professors from two other related departments on campus. They agreed to write letters for him and maintain his confidence. Note that some academics believe it is worth taking a chance to request a letter of recommendation from a member of your current department. If you are able to locate such a colleague, she or he would be able to vouch for your research and teaching, as well as your character as a colleague, and waylay any concerns the search committee may have about your progress in the prospective department more convincingly than you could.

Because you are searching as a more seasoned candidate (e.g., you have been in your current post between two and five years), it is important to have letters from people with more seniority than yourself. So although it was acceptable to have a letter of reference from an assistant professor when you entered the job market as a graduate student, you should now focus on letters of reference from people who are *at least* associate professors. Such people have already earned tenure and established credibility in their arenas. Letters of reference should be provided from people who can vouch for your research, teaching, and potential, people who have strong academic reputations themselves, and people whose disciplines are linked to yours.

Ethics in the Job Search

Search committees are focused on selecting the most qualified candidate who best fits their departmental or program needs. Some applicants who currently hold a tenure-track position may be viewed suspiciously. Even if the committee considers you a potentially strong candidate, some may be wondering, "Why does she/he wish to leave her/his current post"? The question will loom larger if you are currently working at an institution that is considered prestigious, high paying, or where top people in your research area are employed. Because many tenured academics assume that junior scholars are most focused on obtaining tenure, some may wonder why you are attempting to leave an institution *prior* to tenure. Are you a difficult colleague? Not a team player? Are you leaving because you believe you won't earn tenure at your current institution? Are there funding issues or is the department or program experiencing a mass exodus? The search committee may not directly ask such questions, and it is important to know that your application packet will probably be viewed somewhat differently than that of an application from an ABD or a new Ph.D. A search committee member may also learn about your professional and personal performance informally via friends in academia. You would be surprised by the insular nature of most academic disciplines.

The closer you are to tenure, the more suspicious some search committees may be about the legitimacy of your candidacy. Although it is greatly frowned upon, some junior faculty re-enter the job market during their sixth year as a strategy to garner higher salaries at their current institution. Such people apply at another institution, get a job offer at the second institution, and subsequently use that offer to get a substantially higher counteroffer at their current one. This approach is disingenuous because the person had no intention of leaving their current post, misled the second institution, and potentially prevented other (sincere) candidates from being considered. Although this calls into question one's academic ethics, it is a practice that occurs more commonly than some like to acknowledge. If you are re-entering the job market during your sixth year, a search committee may be suspicious about your motives. It is important that you convey your genuine interest in the post (via cover letter) and be sure you are interested as well. The cover letter can also be used to address other potential questions a search committee might have (attempt to "think" like a search committee to address potential issues a priori). Remember, your goal is to convince the committee that you are the best candidate for the position and set to rest any concerns that could undermine their ability to consider you fully.

■ Similarities and Differences in the Job Search Process

Some of the material from earlier chapters will be germane to people re-entering the job market (for example, Chapter 6, onsite visits and negotiating issues). However, because you are currently a faculty member rather than a graduate student entering the market for the first time, search committees will have higher expectations. They will expect you to be more polished and seasoned than a graduate student and to have a more extensive productivity profile. To help increase the likelihood of a successful search, it is important to recognize how this search process is similar—and how it differs—from your first job search as a graduate student.

You should expect to submit an application packet, usually based on an advertisement. However, if you are applying for an associate professor's position, an institution may initially request only a detailed cover letter and curriculum vita. In such instances, additional material and supporting documentation (such as a teaching portfolio) will be requested only from a shorter list of the most viable candidates. Be sure to include only the requested items (if only contact names for references are requested, do not send actual letters). You may learn about a potential position that has yet to be formally advertised. In such instances, you may be asked to mail a cover letter and vita to a specific person within the department so that an initial informal review of your credentials can be made. It is important to consider this a preliminary phase— expect the formal application process to follow. The more advanced the position for which you are applying, the more you should expect requests for official documentation of published articles and books, grant documentation, teaching reviews, and other awards. Do not be surprised by additional levels of contact by a search committee.

Once you receive an interview invitation, be open and prepared for a varied interview process and schedule. Again, the more advanced the potential position (such as associate professor or advanced assistant professor), the more detailed and lengthy the interview process may be. Do not let the process become daunting. Remember, when applying for an advanced position, the department has to determine whether you are a strong candidate *and* whether you are qualified to receive tenure upon acceptance or in the near future (in one or two years). As such, expect a thorough, detailed review of your application packet before being invited to campus, and of you during the campus visit.

The type of campus interview may differ based on the type of position. If you are applying for a more advanced position at a research institution, you may be required to provide only a traditional research-oriented job talk and not teach a class. In other cases, you may be required to do both. During a research presentation, be prepared to answer very detailed, pointed questions regarding your research, methods, data, limitations, and where your research fits into the discipline. Although you will be questioned in a fashion similar to that during your graduate student interviews, expect a more intense interview process and higher expectations relative to the thoroughness of your responses and level of self-presentation (search committees are usually more forgiving of guffaws and minor mistakes from less experienced graduate students and newly minted Ph.D.s than they will be from candidates such as yourself who have already started a career in academia). Also be expected to answer questions about why you have re-entered the job market. Prepare a response that focuses on the benefits of continuing your career at the new institution and avoid disparaging remarks about your current position or department.

If you are offered a position, the negotiating process should include the issues presented in Chapter 6. Although newly minted Ph.D.s are often allowed to teach courses they have previously taught while in graduate school, you may now be required to teach certain specialty courses or advanced classes in your research or teaching area. Because you are not a traditionally "new" candidate, institutions will likely have increased research and teaching expectations. If you have not done so, initiate a conversation to determine when your new "tenure clock" will start. If you are accepting a position as a new assistant professor (i.e., starting over), then you will begin at year one. At the other extreme, if you are accepting a position as an associate professor, your prospective department has already confirmed your new rank (be sure to get this decision in writing). Also note the possibility of being offered a position as an untenured associate professor, which typically requires tenure consideration in one to three years.

However, if you are entering the new position as an advanced assistant professor, consensus must be determined regarding when you will be evaluated for tenure in your new post. This conversation will usually take place between you and the department chairperson/head (or possibly the dean, depending on the size of the institution and administrative structure) during the overall negotiating process. For example, you may be in year three at your current post and wish to continue as scheduled toward tenure (meaning you would be considered three years into the new position), or you might wish to be considered earlier or possibly later or have a range of years during which you have the latitude to "go up" for tenure. The timing of this decision should be based on when it is objectively believed that you will be ready to be considered for tenure. Your involvement in shaping this decision will be affected by the specific institution, but you should provide input and feel comfortable negotiating a tenure clock start that will maximize your chances of earning tenure when you are considered.

You should spend considerable time thinking about a comprehensive resource package. Remember that an acceptable package reflects the salary as well as other resources required to successfully meet teaching and/or research responsibilities. Your current experiences will provide information about the specific types of resources you will need. Do some research via the Internet and discipline-specific guides regarding the acceptable salary range for assistant and/or associate professors. A profile as an advanced assistant professor will place you between these two ranks, but at least you will have information needed to know whether an offer is acceptable and have data to suggest a counteroffer.

Remember that the ideal time to garner a top salary is during the negotiating process. It is often more challenging to get substantially large pay increases subsequently—most institutions are notorious for salary compression among existing faculty. If the position is for an associate professor, expect a higher salary, but base your expectations on current discipline and institutional guidelines. Although you probably negotiated about general, standard resources during your first job search as a graduate student, your requests should now be more specific (for example, you may require certain computer software to perform research rather than the standard fare typically provided, or certain teaching resources to properly prepare for graduate courses). When negotiating, be sure your professional needs are being addressed (in writing). Also make sure the post provides a balance between your professional and personal requirements (refer to Chapter 8) to increase the likelihood that a move to this new position will be a good one.

Once you have completed negotiations and signed and returned the contract (be sure the contract details *all* agreed upon aspects of your new position), wait until you receive a copy of the contract that has been signed by the appropriate officials at the new institution, then schedule a meeting to inform your department head/chairperson about your decision to change positions. Most decisions about positions are finalized during spring semester (in preparation for new faculty to begin during the subsequent fall). This should give your current department ample time to prepare for your departure (no need to burn bridges by giving late notice) and give you time to relocate. In some cases, if the department does not wish to lose you, a counteroffer may be made—and the new institution may make a subsequent counteroffer. This process can be time consuming and potentially tenuous. If you are certain about your decision to leave, let your current department head/chairperson know that, although you are flattered, a counteroffer is unnecessary. Be sure the meeting with your current department head/chairperson is professional. If you have comments about the position and suggestions for improvements, feel free to discuss them as objectively as possible, especially if you believe your comments may help enhance the department. However, more subjective, overly emotional comments are probably not helpful and should be avoided. And no matter how challenging your stint may have been at the institution, be sure to leave graciously and professionally.

Just as performing a thorough, organized job search will increase the likelihood of locating the ideal position after leaving graduate school, a similar process will help ensure success during subsequent job searches. Pre-tenure searches will require you to understand how the process is similar to your earlier experiences on the job market as well as the nuances of this second search. Again, your objectives should consider professional as well as personal dynamics and be informed by resources such as this book and advice from academic mentors. An informed, proactive search will increase your chances of success in locating a new position that provides opportunities for advancement, stimulating teaching and/or research, and the opportunity to continue to use the experiences you garnered in your initial tenure-track position.

11

Conclusion:
Balancing the Professional
and the Personal

During the academic job search, what are realistic expectations? Should you expect to locate your ideal tenure-track position? An acceptable position? Multiple offers? What should you anticipate in terms of an academic package? In terms of quality of life? What should be your criteria? We would all love a position with a great salary, benefits, perks, unlimited resources, a low teaching load, collegial peers, students excited about learning, and research ideas guaranteed to result in publications. And, of course, this position would be located at an institution in an area with the social resources and community culture conducive to our specific personal needs so that we maximize quality of life for ourselves and our mates and/or children. But in reality, such a position does not exist. Even the best position will not meet all of your professional and personal needs. No position will be perfect and each academic package will involve compromise on your part. Having said that, you must decide how to compromise and under what conditions compromise is unacceptable. So while it is unrealistic to envision a perfect position, it is quite realistic to search for one that meets your required conditions and some of your desired ones. As a candidate, you must have a set of realistic criteria by which you evaluate positions. Without such criteria, you will be unable to objectively and succinctly compare and contrast your options and select one that is best for you.

It should be evident that taking part in a successful job search will entail considering important issues relative to the actual academic package and equally important nonacademic issues. This means being able to make decisions throughout the application process, being able to make a final decision about an offer, and being able to live with the consequences of your decisions. This also means making decisions based on as much information as is available and taking ownership of the information-gathering process (remember the advice given to me—when all is said and done, only you will be looking out for you). A variety of ideas, suggestions, and tips have been included in this book to help you organize and structure your job search. However, at the heart of this process will be several basic questions for each prospective position: Will I be able to teach and/or perform research in this position, that is, can I do the job for which I've been trained here? Can I be happy here? Do I feel good about the position and the place? Will my partner, spouse, and/or children feel similarly? Will accepting this job meet my important professional and personal goals and needs? Have I gotten enough information to make an informed decision? Balancing the professional and personal dimensions of your search may seem challenging, but with the appropriate structure to guide the process and consideration based on objective (and in some cases, subjective) criteria, you will increase the chances of locating the desired position. The goal of this book is to provide you with information to make the best choice when considering opportunities. There are no guarantees that going through a structured search process will result in your locating employment, or that, if you locate a post, it will be ideal. However, by proactively organizing and planning your academic search, you will increase the chances of locating the academic position that is both professionally and personally ideal for you.

Index

Academic climate, and personal fit, 152–154

Academic fit. *See* Professional fit

Academic job market. *See* Job market

Advertisements, examples of, 46, 47–53. *See also* Application process

Application packet: contents of, 43, 57; development of, 57–81; importance of, 57; tracking of, 81, 82; types of accomplishments to highlight in, 80–81; writing samples and supporting documents in, 79–80. *See also specific document*

Application process, 43–82; academic- and personal-fit considerations in, 55–56; and applications to prestigious institutions, 45; bulleted posting in, 50–51; for expanded job search, 135–136; financial considerations in, 56; general traits needed for success in, 6–9; importance of following instructions in, 45–46; and job posting respons-

es, 45–53; letter of recommendation in, 13–14, 16–18; and pre-application decisions, 44–45; review and editing of documents in, 14; and school selection issues, 44–45; summarized posting in, 49; tenure considerations in, 56

Career choices, faculty advice on, 14

Conference interviews: benefits of, 104; as initial screening process, 103–104; postconference follow-up on, 106–107; preparations for, 104–106

Conferences and meetings, benefits of participating in, 34–35

Cover letter: elements of, 59; faculty reviews of, 58; and job market re-entry, 188–191; marketing function of, 58; preparation of, 57–58; publishing accomplishments listed in, 190; samples of, 60–66; teaching performance details in, 190–191

Curriculum vita: content and devel-

ed career timeline, 159–160; family relocation issues in, 156–157, 161; new locale characteristics and, 160–161, 163–164; and nontraditional candidates' concerns, 166–168; and personal needs and requirements, 160–161; and spousal hiring, 156–159; subjective meaning of, 150–151. *See also* Personal fit

Religion, as job search issue, 166
Research institution, sample application cover letter for, 64–66
Research opportunities: in joint positions, 138; for nontraditional candidates, 177–178; in postdocs and fellowships, 144

Search committees: application requests of, 67; candidate selection process of, 53–54; lists, 54–55; types of issues considered by, 55–57; "unstated" rules of, 21
Senior faculty, establishing ties with, 17
Service: experience, included in curriculum vita, 70; as new faculty requirement, 56
Sexual orientation, as job search consideration, 166–167. *See also* Nontraditional candidates
Social skills: opportunities for developing, 34; and self-presentation in interviews, 122–126
Spousal hiring, 156–159
Student accomplishments, portfolio presentation and, 99
Student evaluations, presentation of, 97–98

Teaching effectiveness, evidence of, 97–99
Teaching institutions: application cover letter for, 60–62; sample advertisement from, 47–48
Teaching philosophy statement, 87–88, 90
Teaching portfolio, 83–102; appendices, content of, 101; benefits of, 84–86; components of, 87–101; concept of, 83; curriculum vita inclusion in, 101; and determination of good fit, 86; future teaching goals and plans presented in, 100; importance of flow in, 87; official teaching evaluation letter in, 14; outside consultants for developing, 84; personal educational philosophy in, 87–89; and personal pedagogy development, 85–86; presentation, 87; principles for constructing, 86–87; sample table of contents for, 88*fig;* student accomplishment evidence in, 99; teaching effectiveness documentation in, 85, 96–99; teaching evaluations in, 96–99; teaching materials in, 96; teaching responsibilities statement in, 93–96; teaching-related activities documented in, 99–100; writing style in, 87
Teaching presentation, in onsite job interview, 115–117
Teaching responsibilities statement, development of, 93–96
Teaching skills: faculty critique of, 14; in research-oriented institutions, 33
Teaching statement: defined,

About the Book

Sandra Barnes presents both big-picture strategic thinking and nuts-and-bolts suggestions to help junior scholars obtain satisfying academic employment in today's highly competitive market. Noteworthy features of *On the Market* include:

- easy-to-read checklists for navigating the search process
- clues to "reading between the lines" of job postings
- practical advice on preparing the "paperwork": CVs, teaching portfolios, conference papers, journal articles, etc.
- no-nonsense tips—the "dos and don'ts"—for a variety of interview settings
- frank discussion of both the professional *and* the personal aspects of any job search
- attention to the concerns of nontraditional and underrepresented groups
- guidance for untenured scholars who want to switch jobs

Written in a straightforward and pragmatic manner, this rich resource will help scholars identify their ideal job—and then land it.

Sandra L. Barnes is associate professor in the Department of Sociology at Case Western Reserve University in Cleveland, Ohio. Previously, she was a joint-appointed associate professor in the Sociology and Anthropology Department and the African American Studies Research Center at Purdue University. In addition to traditional academic publications, she has numerous self-help and general topic publications in mainstream magazines.